DISCOVER IRISH ART AT THE NATIONAL GALLERY OF IRELAND

DISCOVER IRISH ART

AT THE NATIONAL GALLERY OF IRELAND

A REFERENCE BOOK ON IRISH ART

Marie Bourke and Síghle Bhreathnach-Lynch

National Gallery of Ireland Gailearaí Náisiúnta na hÉireann

Published in 1999 by
The National Gallery of Ireland
Merrion Square West
Dublin 2

Text copyright © Marie Bourke, Síghle Bhreathnach-Lynch and the National Gallery of Ireland, 1999

Supported by The Department of Education and Science, and The Gulbenkian Foundation

British Library Cataloguing in Publication Data available

ISBN: 0903162822

Note
Paintings in this book are arranged in chronological order
to illustrate developments in the history of Irish art.
Dimensions are given height before width.
Abbreviations
NGI No. refers to the National Gallery of Ireland's Inventory number
for the work of art in the Collection.
RA – Royal Academy
RHA – Royal Hibernian Academy

Front Cover: *Loch an Mhuilinn*, Charles Lamb (1893-1964)
Frontispiece: *The Cock*, Evie Hone (1894-1955)
Title Page illus.: *Self-Portrait*, Leo Whelan (1892-1956)
Back Cover: *The Piping Boy*, Nathaniel Hone the Elder (1718-84)

Text Editor: Elaine Campion
Index: Helen Litton
Design: Bill Bolger
Photography: Roy Hewson
Rights & Reproductions: Marie McFeeley
Printed in Ireland by ßetaprint Ltd, Dublin

Contents

Authors' Acknowledgements

The authors would like to express their appreciation to the following people:

At the National Gallery of Ireland, Raymond Keaveney, Director, Dr Hilary Pyle, Yeats Curator, Anne Stewart, Senior Researcher, Elizabeth Player, Registrar, Niamh McGuinne, Conservator, Marie McFeeley, Rights and Reproductions Officer, Roy Hewson, Photographer, Elizabeth Coman, Education Administrator, Marion McEnroy, Education Department, Marie Fitzgerald, Gallery Shop/Publications Manager, Vivienne Lynch, Finance Officer, Attendants' Hanging Party: Paul Irwin, Ken Nicoletti and Martin Irwin.

To Jane MacAvock, Curator of Prints and Drawings, who helped select the set of slides provided to accompany a limited edition of *Discover Irish Art: Teacher's Resource Pack*, copies of which have been distributed to primary and post-primary schools in the thirty-two counties, with the assistance of the Department of Education and Science.

We are deeply indebted to a number of other people: Professor Anne Crookshank, Professor John Turpin, Professor Kenneth McConkey, Mary Pat O'Malley and Brendan Rooney.

The authors would like to record a particular note of appreciation to Micheál Martin TD, Minister for Education and Science, and John Dennehy, Secretary General of the Department of Education and Science, for the support provided for this book.

Thanks to the Gulbenkian Foundation, notably Ben Whitaker, the Director, for the sustained support of education activities during the past decade.

Le míle buíochas.

Copyright Acknowledgements

Foreword

IN ADDITION TO its magnificent collection of European old master paintings, the National Gallery of Ireland possesses an unrivalled collection of Irish art, ranging in date from about 1700 to virtually the present day. While there is a superb range of reference material available on the old masters, there is very little information in published form on Irish artists, particularly in respect of the lesser known individuals.

Discover Irish Art, which casts a wide view over the Gallery's Irish Collection, has been written to fill this void. It seeks to provide visitors, particularly teachers and students, and indeed anyone interested in Irish art, with a ready guide to the Collection. Each illustration is accompanied by a concise commentary on the artist's career and the work reproduced. As the paintings are in chronological order, one can read through the complete text and get a sense of the development of Irish art down through the centuries as it reflects its own unique cultural identity, against the backdrop of developments elsewhere in Europe.

Thanks to the generous support of the Department of Education and Science and the Gulbenkian Foundation, this publication will be distributed to every school in Ireland, providing teachers and students with a rich and varied introduction to an aspect of their national heritage.

Raymond Keaveney
Director

Preface

As we move into the twenty-first century, we find ourselves reflecting on the breadth and achievement of our Irish cultural heritage. For a nation that has a great wealth of talent in its verbal, musical and literary traditions, *Discover Irish Art* testifies to the depth and extent of creativity in our visual arts.

If we step back in time we can see that the visual tradition has tangible roots in prehistory. Irish art and achievement date back to the Neolithic period (c.3000-2000 BC), when pre-historic people carved images and markings on stone monuments, forming graves and burial chambers. The most significant art of the Neolithic period was produced by people associated with the Irish passage-grave cemeteries in the Boyne Valley, at Knowth, Dowth and Newgrange. The triple-spiral and other patterned ornaments decorated on the stones, or megaliths, which archaeologists and art historians continue to try to decipher, are examples of the potent imagery that has been influential in Irish art down to the present day. The Early Christian period produced great Irish artists, whose work is evidenced in a variety of art forms: scribes and illustrators who produced books of the artistic calibre of The Book of Kells; accomplished metalworkers, among them the creators of the Tara Brooch and the Ardagh Chalice; unnamed sculptors responsible for carving magnificent high crosses, such as those at Ahenny, Co. Tipperary, Monasterboice, Co. Louth, and Clonmacnoise, Co. Offaly. The extraordinary standard and accomplishment of these early Irish artists' work was followed during the Norman period and later in medieval Gaelic Ireland by the setting up of monastic orders and the building of great religious founda-tions displaying well-designed architecture, intricate carvings and some murals, most of which have since disappeared. Examples include St Cormac's Chapel, Cashel, Co. Tipperary, Clonfert Cathedral, Co. Galway, Mellifont Abbey, Co. Louth, and St Patrick's Cathedral in Dublin. The quality, assurance and competence of these anonymous artists continued over successive periods up to the late seventeenth century and early eighteenth century, when it is again evidenced in the work of silversmiths, plasterworkers and stuccoers who worked in the great country houses and fashionable Dublin buildings. This book takes up the story of the Irish creative tradition, beginning when panel painting first appeared in Ireland in the late seventeenth century, and continuing through three centuries to the mod-ern movements of the twentieth century.

The Department of Education and Science sees its role as supporting and extending the concept of education as a process of lifelong learning. In this respect the National Gallery of Ireland has worked in association with the Department in devising high-quality art materials. In recent times there has been sustained growth in the area of the visual arts, and the Department has been applying its resources to make provisions for changes in the area of art curriculum development. While the success of the new art curriculum at Junior Certificate level is well documented, the Department is addressing the task of devising a related art curriculum for the Leaving Certificate. The next priority under consideration is devising a coherent and co-ordinated art curriculum for primary level, in conjunction with post-primary developments. In this way, the Department is making every effort to raise the standard of art education in Ireland in tandem with the new awareness and growth in the visual arts.

Discover Irish Art has been written as a reference book on Irish art, not just for teachers, but for anyone who is interested in the Irish visual art tradition. The Department of Education and Science is proud to be associated with a resource book of this standard of excellence. The hundred works of Irish art from the National Gallery of Ireland illustrated in the book offer a unique perspective on the emergence of the visual arts in Ireland. The authors, Marie Bourke, Keeper and Head of Education, and Síghle Bhreathnach-Lynch, Curator of the Irish Collection, bring great scholarship and experience to the writing of this book. They balance this with a measured assessment of the most appropriate works to reflect the development of Irish art from the late seventeenth to the twentieth century. They are to be commended for the enthusiasm and energy they have put into the book, and encouraged to continue their research into the world of Irish art. I hope *Discover Irish Art* helps Irish people to acknowledge and recognise the value of their native art.

Micheál Martin, TD
Minister for Education and Science

About this Book...

*D*iscover *Irish Art* is a reference book on the history of Irish art, viewed through the lens of one hundred works of art in the Irish Collection of the National Gallery of Ireland. The idea for the book came from members of the public, teachers, and adults attending the Gallery's Art Studies programmes, who have constantly asked if a guide to the Irish Collection could be devised that would also chart the history of Irish art.

Anyone who has an interest in Irish art will be familiar with the standard reference books, most of which have been published within the past thirty years. Charting the history of Irish art, therefore, is a relatively new subject and so it is worth recording some of these books because they have provided almost the only available source of information. The most well known is Walter Strickland's *Dictionary of Irish Artists*, published in 1913. In 1969 Anne Crookshank and the Knight of Glin, Desmond FitzGerald, published *Irish Portraits 1660-1860*, and Bruce Arnold published *A Concise History of Irish Art*. Anne Crookshank and the Knight of Glin then published more comprehensive material on Irish art, *The Painters of Ireland* (1978) and *The Watercolours of Ireland* (1994). National Gallery of Ireland publications included Michael Wynne's *Fifty Irish Painters*, published in 1983, and the following year Julian Campbell's *The Irish Impressionists*. 1984 saw the launch of the *Irish Arts Review* (renamed *Irish Arts Review Yearbook*) which documents new research in art history. A book dealing with more modern periods was published in 1991 by S. B. Kennedy, entitled *Irish Art and Modernism 1880-1950*. Valuable research material has been provided by Anne Stewart's *Royal Hibernian Academy of Arts, Index of Exhibitors 1826-1976* (1985 and 1987); *Irish Art Loan Exhibitions 1765-1927, Index of Artists* (1990); *Irish Societies and Sketching Clubs 1870-1980* (1997). More recently Brian Kennedy's *Irish Painting* was published in 1993, Catherine Marshall's *Irish Art Masterpieces* in 1994 and *Modern Art in Ireland* by Dorothy Walker in 1997. Articles on contemporary Irish art are published in *Circa*, complemented by biographies of modern Irish artists published by Gandon Editions.

Research on Irish art is now established practice, promoted in Art History departments in Dublin at University College, Trinity College, the National College of Art and Design, at the National Gallery of Ireland, Irish Museum of Modern Art, Royal Hibernian Academy Gallagher Gallery, Hugh Lane Municipal Gallery of Modern Art, at the Institute of Irish Studies, Queen's University, the University of Ulster, and the Ulster Museum in Belfast, the School of Art and Design and Hunt Museum in Limerick, the Crawford Municipal Art Gallery and School of Art in Cork, and through the Open University. Interesting material on Irish art is emerging from other third-level colleges, appearing in an interdisciplinary form, and there is much worthwhile scholarship in the field of Irish art being carried out overseas.

Discover Irish Art turned out to be a labour of love. There was great joy in being able to include wonderful works of art and a sense of loss at having to leave out others. Endless time was spent looking carefully at each work of art, researching its history, following up interesting suggestions, making new discoveries, discussing thoughts and ideas with other colleagues in the field, and finally putting pen to paper. In the writing of this book we have learnt so much more about Ireland's history, heritage and visual art tradition. It is a rich story to tell as it unfolds. We hope audiences gain as much enjoyment from reading it as we obtained in the research and writing.

Marie Bourke and Síghle Bhreathnach-Lynch

List of Illustrations

IN ORDER OF APPEARANCE

Introduction

*D*iscover Irish Art celebrates the extraordinary range and excellence of the Irish art tradition. Irish literary culture is well known — everywhere we turn we see images of Shaw, Yeats, Joyce, Beckett and Heaney, all major figures praised for their achievements in the field of literature. In this book, one hundred beautiful images offer a unique perspective on the rich heritage of Irish culture expressed by notable artists such as Latham, Barry, Ashford, Mulready, Osborne and Henry, whose creative achievements have influenced their own as well as succeeding generations. Many of these artists have produced accomplished and technically brilliant works, which are a source of inspiration, pleasure and enjoyment for so many people. *Discover Irish Art* acknowledges and celebrates this achievement. It contains illustrations of some great works, which invite observation and study: from an outstanding subject painting *The Conjurer* by Nathaniel Hone the Elder, to breathtaking landscapes by Thomas Roberts, such as *Lucan House and Demesne*; from the masterpiece *Frederick Hervey, Bishop of Derry and Fourth Earl of Bristol with his Granddaughter Lady Caroline Crichton, in the Gardens of the Villa Borghese, Rome* by Hugh Douglas Hamilton, to the neo-classical image of *Hibernia with a Bust of Lord Cloncurry* by John Hogan; the magnificent sweep of history in *The Marriage of Princess Aoife with Strongbow* by Daniel Maclise, to the romance of *The Meeting on the Turret Stairs* by Frederic William Burton; from a humorous anecdotal theme in *Military Manoeuvres* by Richard Moynan, to the delightful *Preliminary Investigation* by Mildred Anne Butler; Orpen's complex satire on Ireland, *The Holy Well*, to John Lavery's brilliant observation of his family in *The Artist's Studio*; an exquisite, bejewelled vision of *The Song of the Mad Prince* by Harry Clarke, to a cubist-inspired *Decoration* by Mainie Jellett; from the narrative and expressive brush of Jack B. Yeats' *The Singing Horseman*, to the more austere style of his niece Anne in *Women and Washing, Sicily*.

An original essay accompanies each of the works of art, providing an historical perspective and illuminating the appropriate political, economic, social and cultural environment. A chart outlining Irish artists over the centuries is provided at the end of the book.

Discover Irish Art is a reference book which will make the sweep of developments in art through the centuries easier to follow, starting with the portrait of *Ladies Catherine and Charlotte Talbot* painted by John Michael Wright in 1679 and crossing three centuries to conclude with the *Portrait of Noel Browne* painted in 1985 by Robert Ballagh, a contemporary artist. These works of art are significant for a number of reasons: they illustrate the extent and variety of work being produced in Ireland — portrait miniatures, paintings, sculpture, drawings, watercolours and stained glass; they reaffirm a pattern of imagination and intense creativity in the visual arts that has continued from earlier periods in history; they provide clear evidence of a visual expression that is as much a part of the national psyche as verbal, musical or literary expression. *Discover Irish Art* is about recognising the value of our native art.

Figure 1
William Congreve,
Godfrey Kneller

LATE SEVENTEENTH-AND EIGHTEENTH-CENTURY IRISH ART

The history of modern painting in Ireland has its roots in the seventeenth century. The lack of a settled political economy in preceding centuries had done little to attract visiting artists to Ireland and very few indigenous painters can be traced. During the peace that followed King Charles II's accession to the throne, the fine arts began to grow in Ireland. The first viceroy of the Restoration, James Butler, First Duke of Ormonde, was a patron of the arts, and in furnishing his castle at Kilkenny with fine tapestries, furniture and paintings, he set a trend for others to follow. His viceroyalty also brought a time of prosperity to Dublin. Between 1660 and 1685 the population doubled, expansive building schemes were initiated and the city attracted artists and craftworkers who saw opportunities opening up for them.

With the defeat of King James II at the Battle of the Boyne in 1690, the dominance of the Protestant Ascendancy class in Ireland was firmly established, and many landlords amassed wealth and kept abreast of styles and fashions in London. In the eighteenth century they built new houses to reflect their affluence and invited painters to make records of themselves and their property. The earliest known Irish paintings are portraits and many of the painters were either trained in the Low Countries or were taught by artists who had trained there. Garret Morphy, about whom little is known, was the first Irish-born artist of consequence to be favoured by these new patrons of the arts. He was a Catholic and many of his commissions came from Jacobite families in Ireland, even after the Battle of the Boyne, though after that date many settlers were included among his patrons. His portraits, marked with precise, realistic detail of textures, show the influence of Flemish as well as English painters.

For political and social reasons there was much contact with England. Although quite a number of the earlier painters were British-born, many made their careers in Ireland. One of them was John Michael Wright, who lived for a few years in Ireland during the late 1670s. Artists of note like Charles Jervas, born in Co. Offaly, travelled to London and visited Dublin from time to time. Having trained under Godfrey Kneller (Fig. 1), who held the position of painter to King George I, Jervas succeeded him in the post. The leading resident portraitist of the first half of the eighteenth century was James Latham, from Co. Tipperary, who studied abroad and developed a sophisticated style based on continental influences. Stephen Slaughter, an English artist who also trained under Kneller, paid several visits to Ireland, painting exquisitely wrought portraits which document contemporary tastes in fashion among the well-to-do Irish landed families (Fig. 2). During the period

Figure 2
A Lady and Child,
Stephen Slaughter

circa 1700-1850, the miniature portrait became a highly popular art form in Ireland, with miniaturists working in enamel and watercolour on ivory. In the mid eighteenth century a group of distinguished miniaturists, including Nathaniel Hone the Elder, Horace Hone, Thomas Frye and Adam Buck, established Dublin as a centre for miniature painting. The late eighteenth century also saw a number of highly talented Irish portrait painters and painters in oils, among them Robert Hunter and Hugh Douglas Hamilton.

An important development during the eighteenth century was that of landscape painting. Two landscapists of note at the beginning of the century are Francis Place and William van der Hagen. Place, a traveller and antiquary from the north of England, arrived in Drogheda in 1698 and travelled to Dublin, then to Waterford, via Kilkenny. His views are noted for their topographical accuracy and clarity (Fig. 3). Van der Hagen came to Ireland about 1722/3 and painted a number of port scenes, classical landscapes, imaginary views and decorative works, bringing a more fanciful, idyllic landscape to the country. From their work, two strands developed: topographical views and idealised landscapes. Jonathan Fisher was the leading exponent of topographical painting, and the National Gallery of Ireland possesses several paintings by him of scenic views in Co. Kerry, as well as aquatints of places of interest in Dublin. The Dublin artist George Barret is renowned for his spectacular views of Co. Wicklow. Meanwhile, Robert Carver, Thomas Roberts and William Ashford painted topographical views and also idealised, imaginary landscapes. These landscapes, in the manner of Claude, Vernet and Dutch artists, are remarkable for their carefully structured compositions and their idyllic, tranquil mood (Fig. 4).

The eighteenth century also saw the setting up of the Dublin Society Schools in the late 1740s, which enabled those considering a career in the arts and crafts to be trained more easily in Ireland. The leading teacher was Robert West, and instruction at the School focused on drawing, mainly in chalk. Meanwhile in London, Nathaniel Hone the Elder and George Barret were among those artists involved in the establishment of the Royal Academy in 1768. Another foundation member was James Barry of Cork, who was the most important history painter of the age. A difficult man, he became Professor of Painting at the Royal Academy but was expelled for his bitter attacks on fellow members.

Figure 3
*Dublin from the
Wooden Bridge,*
Francis Place

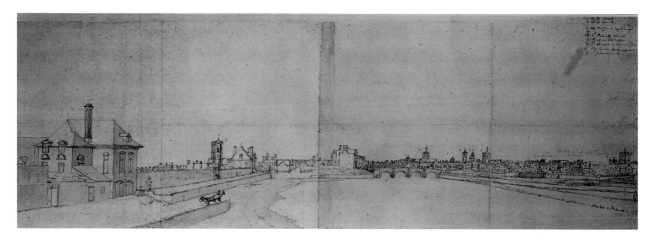

Figure 4
A Landscape,
Thomas Roberts

During the eighteenth century there was a further blossoming of the arts in the areas of architecture and sculpture. Dublin developed and expanded enormously during the reign of the Georges, new ideas in design and planning were put into practice and the building boom was instrumental in creating new urban spaces. A return to the fundamental ideas of ancient classical buildings proved to be a common source of inspiration in their design. Examples include the Custom House (1781), designed by James Gandon, and the Casino at Marino (1762), an exquisite villa built by Lord Charlemont and designed by Sir William Chambers. Sculpture was used in architecture for decorative purposes as well as for the usual portrait and public monument commissions. The most renowned sculpting family of the period was the Smyth family of Dublin. Edward Smyth carried out some of the carvings on the Custom House, where his allegorical heads depicting the rivers of Ireland on the façade are impressive for their vigorous and dynamic carving. The National Gallery of Ireland possesses a portrait bust of George III, produced by Edward and his son John (Fig. 5). The eighteenth century is notable too for trips to the Continent. 'Grand Tours' were undertaken by wealthy Irish gentry, with Rome as the climax; paintings and antiques were acquired on these tours for their town houses and country estates.

DEVELOPMENTS IN THE NINETEENTH CENTURY

The passing of the Act of Union in 1800 resulted in Dublin being no longer the centre of parliamentary government. With the exodus to London of those involved in politics, and their families, a number of Irish artists, including James Arthur O'Connor and Francis Danby, went abroad to work. While the aristocracy had been strong patrons of the arts in Ireland in the previous century, a new type of patron, notably the emerging Protestant

Figure 5
*George III, King of
England,*
Edward Smyth and
John Smyth

professional class, was making an appearance. Following Catholic Emancipation in 1829, a prosperous Catholic merchant class also emerged, but its interest in the arts was to develop more slowly.

The most significant event for Irish artists in the early part of the century was the setting up of the Royal Hibernian Academy in 1823, based on the same principles as those of the Royal Academy in London. The RHA ensured a home-based exhibition venue from 1826 onward and also increased the possibilities of commissions. It established classes in drawing and painting from the antique and from life. The Royal Dublin Society Schools were taken over by the Government in 1849, and in 1877 they were renamed the Metropolitan School of Art, now the National College of Art and Design. Another landmark in 1854 was the Act of Parliament establishing the National Gallery of Ireland, which opened to the public ten years later. In Cork, the Crawford Municipal Gallery opened its doors to the public in 1885, while in Belfast a new school of art was established in 1870. In 1890 the United Sketching Club became the Belfast Art Society. Sustained pressure from art clubs and societies in Belfast resulted in the setting up of the first public gallery there in 1890.

This was a century that saw further growth and development in ideas of national identity, and the emergence of the Young Ireland movement. It was the age of Daniel O'Connell,

Thomas Davis and later of Charles Stewart Parnell; the National Gallery of Ireland possesses portraits of all three men in a variety of media. It was a time marked significantly by famine and emigration on a large scale and, as the century progressed, land agitation became an issue of increasing urgency. Interestingly, few Irish artists tackled these contemporary political themes, and of those who did, the interpretation reduced the harrowing realities of such events to a minimum. Fine art, it was believed, should not overly concern itself with distressing aspects of life. Where contemporary political events were portrayed, a sentimental treatment of the subject prevailed or, conversely, a sense of reportage (Fig. 6). The absence of accurate, objective narrative paintings from this period provides a notable gap in the history of nineteenth-century Irish art. That gap was filled in a different way by magazines such as *The Illustrated London News*, whose detailed commentaries on what was happening in Ireland were accompanied by graphic illustrations drawn by artists.

Paintings of everyday life were a popular category of art throughout this century. Of the earlier genre painters, William Mulready is important for his charming pictures of daily life, which were much admired by British art lovers (Fig. 7). Meanwhile Daniel Maclise, a very versatile and accomplished painter, produced some fine serious documentary and historical paintings, the best known of which is his *Marriage of Princess Aoife with Strongbow*. Frederic Burton was a gifted watercolourist, whose portraits, early Irish subject pictures and landscapes gave way to a later style, illustrated in romantic scenes, similar to the works of the Pre-Raphaelite Brotherhood in England.

Figure 6
The O'Connell Centenary Celebrations,
Charles Russell

Figure 7
Idle Boys,
William Mulready

Throughout the century the demand for portraiture remained constant. Of the portraitists, Martin Archer Shee and Martin Cregan were pre-eminent in the early years of the century. The National Gallery of Ireland has six Cregan paintings, including a delightful *Portrait of Mrs Cregan* (Fig. 8). From mid century, an increasing popularity for anecdote and putting across a moral message is evident in some portraits. A fine example of a modern morality subject in the Victorian tradition is Joseph Haverty's painting, which includes a portrait of the temperance leader, Father Mathew, who is shown receiving a repentant pledge-breaker surrounded by his supportive family (Fig. 9).

Perhaps the most exciting development in Irish art during the nineteenth century was in landscape painting. The majority of Irish landscape artists during the late eighteenth and

Figure 8
Portrait of Mrs
Cregan,
Martin Cregan

Figure 9
Father Mathew
Receiving a Repentant
Pledge-Breaker,
Joseph Haverty

early nineteenth centuries were painters in the romantic style. A natural rapport with the landscape produced a response in artists, among them Francis Danby and James Arthur O'Connor. O'Connor in his later work showed a taste for dramatic, brooding surroundings and for the more mysterious or terrifying elements in nature. Some of his landscapes focus on a stirring interpretation of stormy skies, plunging ravines, fast-flowing rivers and windswept roads (Fig. 10). Topographical landscapes by artists like George Petrie, especially of well-frequented picturesque spots, remained popular throughout the century, and these were often used in guidebooks and map-making. Scenes of Glendalough, Co. Wicklow, were sought after, as were other beauty spots and places of historic interest, like Powerscourt, Co. Wicklow, Leixlip, Co. Kildare and Clonmacnoise, Co. Offaly. Ireland being an island, much of Irish life is associated with the sea. Not surprisingly, marine painting gained popularity, providing opportunities for artistic, romantic effects, dramatic storms and rescues.

By the 1880s, young Irish artists were less inclined to go to London and more interested in centres like Paris and Antwerp. Although the Metropolitan School of Art (a continuation of the Royal Dublin Society Schools of Art after 1877) and the Royal Hibernian Academy Schools offered a solid basis for training, artists were keen to travel to foreign landscapes. In France they were influenced by the *plein-air* painting of the Barbizon School, impressionism and post-impressionism. Nathaniel Hone the Younger applied his experience of painting directly before nature, learned at Barbizon, to his Irish views when he returned home, producing marvellous scenes in which the light and atmospheric changes in Irish

Figure 10
A View of the Devil's Glen, James Arthur O'Connor

weather are strikingly captured in paint. Fired with enthusiasm, painters such as Frank O'Meara, Aloysius O'Kelly and Henry Jones Thaddeus followed exciting new paths of development. Of the painting done abroad by these travelling artists, John Lavery's idyllic scenes, painted in Brittany, Tangiers and London, together with fashionable society portraits, show his absorption of impressionist and other influences, making him one of the leading international artists of his generation. Walter Osborne's records of Dublin life, painted in the 1890s, demonstrate how well he had absorbed the impressionists' concern with effects of light and shadow, if not their methods of painting (Fig. 11). Helen Mabel Trevor and Joseph Malachy Kavanagh both chronicled in paint the places and people they visited; Trevor's images of Breton peasant women are memorable for their sharp observation of character and personality (Fig. 12). One artist, Roderic O'Conor, remained in France, and the early advances of modernism are detectable as an enriching source of inspiration in his work.

Figure 11
A Scene in the Phoenix Park,
Walter Osborne

Changes in sculpture are notable too in this century. There was a shift in the treatment of figurative sculpture, with the purer, ideal, classically sculpted forms of the previous age gradually giving way to a greater interest in naturalism. The statuary of Thomas Farrell, for example his portrayal of William Dargan of 1863, demonstrates the beginnings of this

Figure 12
The Fisherman's Mother,
Helen Mabel Trevor

move towards naturalism, in spite of its smooth, neo-classical surfaces. By the turn of the new century, sculptors such as John Hughes and Oliver Sheppard were at pains to introduce a greater emphasis on naturalism in their sculpted work.

DEVELOPMENTS IN THE TWENTIETH CENTURY

Painters who studied abroad continued to produce innovative work in the new century. William Leech, for instance, spent time in Brittany where, enriched by his contacts with avant-garde art, he proceeded to produce a series of dazzling painterly works, an outstanding example of which is *A Convent Garden, Brittany* (Fig. 13). Jack B. Yeats was the first twentieth-century artist who made Ireland his subject matter, particularly the people, places and folklore he encountered as a boy in Sligo. While he spent time travelling around the country painting images of Irish life and landscape (Fig. 14), his later work is dominated by themes based on memory and past experiences. In these, Yeats' use of colour and impasto, as well as his dynamic, expressive brushwork, create images and moods that make him an outstanding figure in the history of Irish art.

Two artists who turned to the west of Ireland for their subject matter of myth and tradition, were Seán Keating and Paul Henry. Keating was a student of William Orpen, whose teaching at the Metropolitan School of Art in the first decade of the century was very influential on the next generation of Irish artists, and whose own superb portraits are magnificent in both tone value and colour. Keating learned from Orpen the importance of draughtsmanship. He went to the Aran Islands where he painted strong, dramatic compositions of life in the west. Henry spent nearly ten years on Achill, Co. Mayo, and his paintings, which conjure up cloudy skies, thatched cottages and blue and purple mountains, have become synonymous with imagery associated with the west of Ireland.

Figure 13
A Convent Garden,
Brittany,
William Leech

Figure 14
A Cleric,
Jack B. Yeats

In 1920, Henry, Yeats and a few of their contemporaries formed the Society of Dublin Painters so that the more avant-garde artists could display their work. The Society came to represent what was progressive in Irish art, and in this milieu artists could experiment with new ideas. Mainie Jellett first exhibited her cubist and abstract pictures there, as did other modernist artists like Evie Hone and Mary Swanzy (Fig. 15). There were other painters working in the first half of the century who focused their attention on establishing a distinctive school of Irish art; although the origins of this lie in the previous century, with the coming of political independence in 1922 and the setting up of the Free State, they produced a number of memorable images before being overtaken by modernism. The most enduring legacy of this period was to be the evolution of a distinct vision of the landscape, exemplified by Yeats, Henry, Keating, Lamb and MacGonigal. In the field of sculpture, a small number of artists, in particular Albert Power and Oliver Sheppard, tried to produce recognisably Irish art; in the case of Sheppard through his choice of Irish themes, and in that of Power, through a conscious selecting of Irish stone wherever possible. Sculptor Oisín Kelly's subject matter is deeply rooted in Ireland's ancient past, using themes from Celtic folklore. His understanding of form and materials created exciting works which express the essence of that tradition. Meanwhile, those involved in the arts and crafts movement reflected the Celtic Revival to a greater degree than those in the world of fine art. Much use was made of Celtic patterns in the manufacture of furniture, jewellery and other ornamental and embroidery goods.

With the great increase in church building in the nineteenth century, stained glass was in demand. Much of the initial work was designed abroad, however, and was not very exciting. The setting up of classes in the Metropolitan School of Art, under A.E. Child, provided the impetus to raise standards. One pupil, Harry Clarke, developed a refined style which was both highly decorative and imaginative. His use of brilliant colour, creating patterns that glow like precious jewels, had a formative influence, not only on stained-glass artists, but on illustrators and designers alike. A further development in this area was the setting up of An Túr Gloine (the Tower of Glass) in 1903 by Edward Martyn and Sarah Purser. It produced innovative designs of the highest quality. One of the artists who worked there was Evie Hone, who, having trained with Mainie Jellett abroad, started her career as a painter but began working with stained glass in 1933. Her work in this medium was greatly helped by her experience of abstract cubist art, together with her research into medieval Irish carvings and a variety of continental sources. Her expressive painterly style in glass influenced succeeding generations of stained-glass artists.

The establishment of the Irish Exhibition of Living Art in 1943 marked an important watershed in Irish art, because it became a significant annual event, representing the interests of those influenced by international trends. By the late 1950s, internationalism, mainly American in origin, could be detected in the work of many artists. The establishment in 1967 of the international exhibition ROSC (an old Irish word meaning the poetry of vision), brought current works by outstanding artists from all over the world to Dublin, every two to four years, for the next two decades. These influences changed the character of Irish painting and sculpture beyond recognition, introducing a range of styles from abstraction relating to expressionism to colour field painting, and diverse forms of figurative art. New themes also emerged: the 'Troubles' in the north of Ireland have affected artists, while the impact of feminism has also led to a reinterpretation of the female in painting and sculpture.

The works of art in this book have been selected by the authors to illustrate the fact that developments in Irish art over the past three centuries have been extensive, and within the social and political environment are rich in achievement. The scope of the Irish Collection will provide the viewer with an opportunity to follow and better understand the evolution of Irish history and cultural life. The manner in which the Gallery is seeking to involve contemporary artists with the Collection is a new development and something that should inspire further confidence in Irish visual artists. Visitors frequently comment on the strength of the Irish School. It is significant to note that the range and quality of the Irish Collection, which reaffirms patterns of creativity and imagination from the earliest periods, enables us to acknowledge and recognise the value of our native art. The National Gallery of Ireland will continue to acquire the finest works available to record our national art as a precious inheritance for future generations.

Figure 15
Pattern of Rooftops,
Czechoslovakia,
Mary Swanzy

One Hundred Works of Art: *in chronological order*

John Michael Wright (c.1617-94)

THE LADIES CATHERINE AND CHARLOTTE TALBOT 1679

Oil on canvas,
130 x 110 cm
NGI NO. 4184

THIS PORTRAIT of the Talbot children depicts the daughters of Colonel Richard Talbot (1630-91), later Earl and titular Duke of Tyrconnell. Talbot, a Catholic, fought with the royalist forces in the Confederate War (1641-53), narrowly escaping death at Drogheda, Co. Louth. He then served with the future James II in the French and Spanish armies. Following the Restoration of Charles II he emerged as the leading Irish Catholic spokesman at court. He proved to be a shrewd political manipulator. After the accession of James II Talbot, now Earl of Tyrconnell, steadily increased his power. He eventually secured James' agreement not just to the creation of an almost wholly Catholic army and civil administration, but also to preparations for a parliament that would revise the Restoration land settlement. Following the revolution of 1688 Tyrconnell considered making terms with William III, before deciding to hold Ireland for James. After the Battle of the Boyne (July 1690) he advocated a negotiated surrender. However, after the Battle of Aughrim (July 1691) he favoured continued resistance. He died one month later.

Lady Catherine, his daughter, is seated on a chair over which is draped a blue cloak. She is dressed in a fashionable grey French dress of the type worn by upper-class Irish children at the time. It is made of silk, with gold brocade, and has jewelled clasps. Her linen smock is trimmed with needlepoint lace and the gold shoes with red heels are probably French. Her sister, Lady Charlotte, wears a classical-style dress of silk chiffon over cream flannel, with jewelled clasps and pendant pearls. On her feet are Roman sandals. Her long veil of black silk chiffon may be a reference to the death of the children's mother, Katherine Boynton, in 1679, the year the picture was painted. The earl was married again that same year, to the famous beauty Frances Jennings, who was outlawed in 1693 as a dangerous papist but continued to live in Dublin, where she later established a convent. Behind the children can be seen a formal garden. It may represent Carton, the house that was extended by the Duke of Tyrconnell during the 1680s.

The rendering of the textiles and the delicacy of the colours in this portrait show John Michael Wright at the height of his artistic powers. Born in London, Wright trained in Edinburgh with the Scottish artist George Jamesone. In the early 1640s he went to Italy, followed by a few years in France and Flanders, before returning to England in 1656. He worked for both Charles II and the Duke of York. Wright visited Ireland in the late 1670s for two or three years, during which time he painted pictures of a number of aristocratic families, including the Hills, the Kings and various relatives of the Duke of Ormonde. An inscription formerly on the back of this portrait indicates that it was painted in Dublin in 1679. It was intended as a double portrait either for family record purposes or to help the marriage prospects of the two girls (Charlotte married Sir Richard Talbot, styled Viscount Baltinglass and Earl of Tyrconnell in 1702). The luxury of their attire and the background setting would have been seen as indicators of the wealth of the family and thus would have enhanced their chances of marrying well.

Garret Morphy (fl.1650-1716)

WILLIAM, FOURTH VISCOUNT MOLYNEUX OF MARYBOROUGH (c.1655-1717/8) c.1700

Oil on canvas,
74.9 x 61 cm

NGI NO. 4151

THE SITTER, from a noted English Roman Catholic family, is believed to be the third and youngest son of the third Viscount Molyneux, whom he succeeded in 1700. Appointed Collector of Customs at Chester in 1688 by King James II, the viscount was dismissed as a papist when the king, a Catholic, was replaced by the Protestant William III, Prince of Orange. Later, in 1694, he was charged with receiving a colonel's commission from King James, then an exile in France. He was married twice: first to Bridget, daughter and heiress of Robert Lucy of Chalcote. After her death in 1713, he married Mary, daughter of Lieutenant General Bevil Skelton, in 1716.

In this half-length portrait, Molyneux is depicted as quite a young man wearing armour and holding a baton. A creamy white neckcloth, fringed with gold thread, is knotted at his throat and he sports a high, full wig made from white hair of the period around 1700. The portrait is notable for the almost hyper-realism of the texture of the different materials: the hard shine of the armour, the soft material of the scarf, the coarse texture of the wig. The upright stance, serious expression and the hand that firmly holds the baton (note the title *Lord Molyneaux* directly above the baton) lend authority to the figure. The breastplate worn by Viscount Molyneux denotes military leadership and would have been a standard form of recognition. This is a man who commands respect.

Not a great deal is known about the early life of the Irish artist Garret Morphy. He is known to have been in London in 1673, working for the Catholic artist Edmund Ashfield, but it is unclear as to whether or not he had begun his training as an artist in Ireland. Morphy moved about England securing portrait commissions. He moved in mainly Catholic circles and most of his sitters in both countries were from that sector of society. He travelled to Ireland between 1673 and 1694 and may have returned in the late 1680s. His portraits of Irish patrons are most frequent after 1694. In Ireland he was popular as a portrait painter with the so-called Old English, those tightly knit old Catholic families of English origin who had retained their lands during the Reformation and the era of the plantation settlements. Later in his career he painted important English administrators and military leaders in Ireland.

Charles Jervas (c.1675-1739)

PORTRAIT OF A LADY, POSSIBLY LADY MARY WORTLEY MONTAGU (1689-1762) 1720s

Oil on canvas,
214.5 x 126 cm
NGI NO. 4342

THE PORTRAIT illustrated here is thought to be that of the formidable linguist, advocate for women and travel-writer, Lady Mary Wortley Montagu. She is best remembered for the diaries she wrote while accompanying her husband to Constantinople (now Istanbul) when he became British ambassador there in 1716. During her time in Turkey she came across the practice of inoculation against smallpox, which she introduced to England. Revelling in Turkish life, she showed a special interest in the clothes worn by the Turkish people. She admired the fine silks and velvets, the application of embroidery and gold tassels, and the use of sable for lining and trimming. This prompted her to wear such costumes, although it is reported that she nevertheless conformed to the standards of European dress by continuing to wear stays.

This full-length portrait depicts Lady Montagu dressed in Turkish attire, crowned by a fetching head-dress. She is standing gracefully by a keyboard instrument, a clavicytherium, which is an early type of harpsichord. The view behind her is of Constantinople, above whose walls is a profile of the great basilica of Hagia Sophia. This is a flattering portrait of Lady Montagu, as is an almost identical portrait of her by the same artist also in the National Gallery of Ireland. In 1715 she had contracted smallpox, which left her with pocked skin, weak eyesight and no eyelashes.

The artist, Charles Jervas, was a portrait painter and is known to have painted a number of portraits of Lady Montagu during his career. He was born about 1675 in King's County (now Offaly), went to London and is thought to have studied under one of the great portrait painters of the day, Godfrey Kneller (1646/9-1723). From there he went to Italy, returning to London in 1709. According to George Vertue, he did small copies of the Raphael Cartoons. Jervas painted some miniature portraits in oil on canvas, known as 'pictures in little', about 1710. Moving in distinguished literary circles, he portrayed many celebrated contemporaries, such as Alexander Pope, Robert Walpole and Isaac Newton. During several visits to Ireland, he executed portraits of members of the Irish House of Commons. He also painted at least ten portraits of Dean Swift. After Kneller's death in 1723, Jervas was appointed principal painter to King George I, a position he retained under George II. He painted several portraits of George II and the Queen.

James Latham (1696-1747)

BISHOP ROBERT CLAYTON (1695-1758) AND HIS WIFE KATHERINE (née DONNELLAN, d.1766) 1730s

Oil on canvas,
128 x 175 cm
NGI NO. 4370

THIS DOUBLE PORTRAIT of Bishop Robert Clayton and his wife Katherine dates from the early years of their marriage, which took place in 1728. Clayton was successively Bishop of Killala, Bishop of Cork and Ross, and Bishop of Clogher. He travelled extensively on the Continent and was regarded by all who knew him as a man of culture and taste. This particular picture may have hung in his town house in Dublin, on the south side of St Stephen's Green, which is now the headquarters of the Department of Foreign Affairs (it was altered and modified during the nineteenth century). The portrait, painted around the 1730s, depicts the bishop seated at a table holding open a book. It is not clear if the book refers to any particular work – this motif was current in engraved portraits of churchmen at the time. The figure is solidly painted in a realistic manner, distinguished by well-observed details such as the depiction of shadow under the nose and chin area. The billowing clerical robe is lavishly painted in flowing, swirling strokes of paint.

Seated, slightly at a remove from the bishop, is his wife Katherine. Born Katherine Donnellan, she was the daughter of a former lord chief justice of the exchequer. In the manner of portraits of the eighteenth century, and in keeping with prevalent views about women, she is presented as a less forceful personality than her husband. It is her elegance and femininity that are stressed by means of the carefully arranged, graceful pose. Her husband's intellectual prowess, meanwhile, is conveyed in the keen, shrewd expression. The compositional arrangement of the figures is reminiscent of a popular type of portrait of this period, known as the conversation portrait. Such portraits included a number of people, usually in a domestic setting, arranged informally. The figures were small in scale. In this composition the figures are in keeping with more formal portraits. While the bishop is presented against the backdrop of a column, the swathes of red drapery behind the couple help to unify the portrait.

Not a great deal is known about the artist James Latham. Born in Co. Tipperary, he was twenty-eight when he enrolled at the Guild of St Luke in Antwerp (1724), where he remained for one term. He was working in Dublin from 1725. After that, there followed a successful career as a portrait painter in Ireland. The vast majority of Latham's portraits are bust-length and very often painted in oval. He appears to have been an assured and accomplished artist, with a strong feeling for form and character, which helped to make his sitters come alive.

Thomas Frye (1710-62)

SIR CHARLES KEMEYS-TYNTE (1710-85) 1739

Oil on canvas,
127 x 102 cm
NGI NO. 927

SIR CHARLES KEMEYS-TYNTE belonged to a leading English West Country family. The second or third baronet (originally awarded for loyalty to the monarchy), he was among several Tyntes to become members of parliament for Bridgewater. After the death of his brother, Sir John Tynte, in 1740, he succeeded him to the family estate at Goathurst in Somerset. He is known to have collected paintings and devoted much time and interest to laying out the gardens of the family home, Halswell Park, Goathurst. In this splendid three-quarter-length portrait painted in 1739, Sir Charles stands, resplendent, in brown velvet jacket and breeches. His fine wig sheds powder on the shoulders of the jacket. The unbuttoned jacket reveals an eye-catching green satin waistcoat beneath, as well as a fine white shirt complete with frills and neckerchief. A matching hat is tucked under one arm. A sense of the sitter's presence is conveyed by the dark, attentive eyes and stately, elegant pose. While Sir Charles has one hand resting casually on his hip, the other is thrust forward, its long graceful fingers captured in an expressive gesture. His fine bearing suggests that we are in the presence of a man of taste and refinement.

Born in Dublin in 1710, Thomas Frye specialised as a portrait painter. By the early 1730s he had settled in England and was sufficiently highly regarded in his profession to be commissioned by the Saddler's Company in 1736 to paint a portrait of the Perpetual Master, Frederick, the Prince of Wales. The portrait was reproduced as a mezzotint by Frye in 1741. This print technique, in which he excelled, is a process of tone engraving whereby the design is produced by scraping the half-tones and highlights from a specially roughened black-printing surface. A tool called a roper is used for this purpose. What distinguishes mezzotint from other print methods is that the artist works from dark to light, from a black ground to the highlights and not from a white ground to shadows. Due to the quality and the wide circulation of his prints, Frye's work influenced many other artists. He is known to have painted miniature portraits on ivory and on enamel throughout his career and is also reputed to have helped found the Bow porcelain works near London, where he was factory manager for over a decade.

Mary Delany (1700-88)

A YOUNG COUPLE CROSSING A STILE IN A CASTLE GARDEN 1745/6

Ink, pencil and
wash on paper,
36.2 x 46 cm
NGI NO. 2722 (90)

A Young Couple Crossing a Stile in a Castle Garden, from an album of mounted drawings by Mary Delany, is dated 6 March 1745/6 and is similar to other watercolours of the artist's garden at Delville. Delany loved her house and gardens at Delville, in the fashionable Dublin suburb of Glasnevin, where the Botanic Gardens are now located, and she entertained there with style. She was well-connected and her guests, who included the lord lieutenant and many famous personalities of the day, were assured of good company and generous hospitality. The album of watercolours in the National Gallery contains ninety-one sketches executed between 1738 and 1768, similar to the one illustrated here, in pencil, pen and wash. They depict famous houses and gardens in England and scenes of the suburbs of Dublin. In summer, Mary Delany liked to breakfast outdoors in the garden and her day was spent in shellwork, needlework, painting, drawing and seeing that her animals were properly cared for. She did not simply admire the plants that she cultivated in her garden but had botany books to learn all about them. She was concerned with improving the layout and character of the garden, a practice that was widespread in the mid eighteenth century when there was a reaction against the formal garden. These 'improvements' involved creating the appearance of a natural landscape, with winding walks, mounds covered with trees and flowering shrubs, rocks covered with moss, all planted in a wild way so that forest trees and bushes had the appearance of being natural in the environment. These watercolours, illustrating houses and estates, are charming, simple and unpretentious. Their significance today lies in their value as topographical records of gardens, buildings and landscapes, many of which have since been altered or destroyed.

Born in Wiltshire, England, in 1700, Mary Granville was widowed after a short marriage to a Mr Pendarves. During a visit to Ireland in 1731 she met the Reverend Dr Delany, Chancellor of St Patrick's Cathedral, and through him became friendly with Dean Swift. On returning to Dublin in 1743, she married Dr Delany and went to live with him at Delville. One of her first achievements was to use her influence to secure the Deanery of County Down for her husband. After his death she returned to England. She started drawing seriously at the age of thirty and ten years later began painting in oils. She was a pupil of William Hogarth, Bernard Lens and Louis Goupy, the miniature painter. She liked working with others, whether practising shellwork, planning grottos or designing for embroidery. Her major work, the *Hortus Siceus* or *Flora*, for which she made one thousand beautiful flowers from tiny pieces of mosaic paper, was executed when she was between the age of seventy-two and eighty-two. Mary Delany was a remarkable woman, who had a most enterprising career for a lady of her time.

Philip Hussey (1713-83)

AN INTERIOR WITH MEMBERS OF A FAMILY c.1750

Oil on canvas,
62 x 76 cm
NGI NO. 4304

An Interior with Members of a Family is one of the most accomplished paintings attributed to Philip Hussey, an artist from Cloyne, Co. Cork. As a young boy, he went to sea and was shipwrecked on several occasions. His interest in art developed from studying ships' figureheads, and thanks to the patronage of Lord Chancellor Bowes, who noticed his talent, he was able to become a professional painter. While on a visit to England he reputedly copied works by Lely. A talented botanist and musician, Hussey's house in Dublin was a centre for writers and artists of the city. He is known to have carried out portraits for distinguished patrons such as the Leslies, FitzGeralds and O'Briens in south-west Ireland.

This picture, a superb example of a finely observed family group in an interior, is attributed to the artist on stylistic grounds. The family is likely to have been of some significance because they are depicted fashionably dressed in a large, impressive reception room. The picture is most informative about fashion in dress and interiors around 1750. While Hussey's picture shows a classical version of English pillar-and-arch wallpaper, the distinctive form of the fiddle grate and the pattern of the doors give it a more Irish feel. The firescreens on either side of the fireplace feature framed pictures supported on tripods, and were used to prevent a lady's white lead-based make-up from melting before the heat. The carpet is rare at this date and between the two casement windows is a gilded French pier-mirror. Five plain Irish-style Chippendale chairs are placed against the wall. It was the practice in large eighteenth-century Irish houses that chairs were only placed in the centre of a room, around a table, when a meal was to be served, and moved back to their position along the walls when the meal was over. This is a conversation piece, a type of genre painting often described as an informal portrait, showing a group of people in a familiar domestic setting, with an air of recreation. The mid eighteenth century was the great period for this genre in England and it is surprising that conversation pieces were not more common in Ireland.

The family group is stylish and expensively dressed. The father wears a frock-coat with cuffs, waistcoat, knee breeches and a wig. The seated mother wears a crisp blue satin dress and petticoat, the lace stomacher emphasising the low-cut neckline, her fashionable shape achieved through the use of stays and hoop petticoats. The liberal use of lace in her head-dress and ruffles, in addition to the quality of the fabrics worn, emphasise the impression of refinement. The two small girls are presented in a relaxed and informal manner, dressed in linen frocks with headcaps of infancy. In the eighteenth century there was a degree of sensitivity to childhood and to children, which had been lacking in previous centuries. Hussey's picture illustrates the new emphasis on domestic informality that was emerging in the eighteenth century, thus helping to create a sympathetic portrayal of the unknown family.

John Lewis (fl.1740-69)

MARGARET (PEG) WOFFINGTON, ACTRESS (1718-60) 1753

Oil on canvas,
74 x 62 cm
NGI NO. 579

IN THIS DELIGHTFUL oval portrait, the actress Peg Woffington is depicted in three-quarter profile. She is silhouetted against a lightly sketched backdrop of trees, distant hills and sky. Dressed in an elegant mauve silk coat with lace edging and a large soft hat to match, the actress captures the viewer with a thoughtful gaze. Lewis' treatment of the figure, with its porcelain complexion, the careful delineation of the lace and the lightly painted trees in the background, is impressive.

This young woman's life is a story of humble beginnings leading to public adulation on the Dublin and London stages. She was the daughter of a Dublin laundress, and her career began after she was spotted by Madame Violante, manager of a well-known children's theatre group, who first laid eyes on her as she helped her mother with the washing on the banks of the river Poddle. Woffington made her début with Madame Violante, playing a role in a popular play of the period, *The Beggar's Opera*. Described as 'the handsomest woman that ever appeared on the stage', she played a wide variety of parts in Dublin before moving on to London. Becoming a star overnight, she acted in Covent Garden with the most famous actor of the day, David Garrick, and was his mistress for a number of years. She moved in influential circles and enjoyed the respect and friendship of those in high office in Ireland, including the Lord Lieutenant, the Duke of Dorset and the Provost of Trinity College Dublin, Francis Andrews.

Biographical details about the artist are sketchy. He worked as a scene painter at Smock Alley Theatre in Dublin. The theatre was then managed by Thomas Sheridan, father of the dramatist Richard Brinsley Sheridan. Lewis was the first scene painter to be permanently engaged on the staff of a Dublin playhouse. He was responsible for one important innovation, namely, painting a beautiful drop curtain for the theatre in 1757. This was at a time when London theatres had nothing but the usual green curtain. It is known that he painted a number of portraits of theatre people and that he decorated a room at Quilca House, Co. Cavan, for Thomas Sheridan. He also painted a number of landscapes and subject pictures.

Robert Carver (c.1730-91)

LANDSCAPE WITH PEASANTS AND A DOG 1754

Oil on canvas,
128 x 160 cm
NGI NO. 4065

THIS CHARMING SCENE, signed and dated 1754, depicts a landscape bathed in the warm light of a summer's day. In the foreground are trees, rocks and wild undergrowth. A pathway leads towards the fast-flowing river, where three men are in conversation. Close by, a terrier follows a scent towards the water's edge. On the right, trees curve from ground to sky, and on the left a copse of trees occupies the bank above the river. In the distance a blue mountain is visible and the sky is filled with clouds. The palette consists mainly of warm browns and greens. Golden yellows create the effect of strong sunlight. Accents of red, used in the depiction of the clothing of two of the figures, add to the overall richness of tonality.

The scene was painted at a period when there was an expansion of interest in landscape painting in Ireland. Robert Carver is one of a number of artists associated with this development. Coming from a Waterford family of landscape painters, Carver, who was born in Dublin, made his living as a scene painter for the theatre. Taught by his father and Robert West, he is known to have painted scenery from 1754 onward at Smock Alley Theatre in Dublin. He moved to London in 1765 when he became a scene painter in Drury Lane and Covent Garden. He continued to practise as a landscape painter, exhibiting at the Society of Artists in Ireland.

This picturesque image suggests a world of peace and harmony, an ideal world. In fact, that is exactly what the artist has produced in his picture: a place which does not exist but is rather a product of his imagination. This kind of landscape, pioneered in the seventeenth century through the work of the French artists Poussin and Claude, followed by Vernet of the eighteenth century, was formulated to portray idyllic places in tranquil mood. These well-ordered views, receding to a distant horizon, adhere to a set of rules in which alternating areas of light and shadow help to create a sense of distance. Carver uses *coulisses* or wings to frame the picture, a practice devised when painting stage scenery. Representations of real places and views sometimes conformed to this formula. Landscapes such as this, along with visual records of great estates, were very popular with patrons in Ireland, who liked to hang them in the halls and reception rooms of their country and town houses.

Samuel Dixon (c.1745-69)

A BULL-FINCH AND BLUE TIT-MOUSE, WITH PEACHES AND APRICOTS c.1755

Ink and water-
colour on
embossed paper,
30.8 x 40.4 cm
NGI NO. 18298

IT WAS ABOUT 1755 that Samuel Dixon produced sets of embossed pictures of birds and flowers. These pieces were issued in sets of twelve, each one containing a description of the particular flowers or birds and an individual dedication. The watercolour illustrated here is dedicated to the Countess of Kildare. Dixon claimed to have invented the 'basso-relievo' technique, which involved impressing the drawings on coarse grey paper using copper plates so that the design was made to stand out in relief. The watercolours were very popular with collectors. The first set focused on the subject of flowers and was issued in 1748. The success of this venture led him to issue another set in about 1749/50 on the theme of foreign birds, based on plates from George Edward's *Natural History of Uncommon Birds* (1743). Success soon produced imitators, and in order to prevent impostors, Dixon dedicated the 1750 set to the Earl of Meath.

In 1755 Dixon produced a third set of twelve watercolours, and to avoid forgeries he dedicated each one to a notable person and provided a description of the picture on the reverse. The work illustrated here comes from the third and apparently last set devoted to foreign and domestic birds, dated about 1755. It is a most attractive and appealing work. The complete set consisted of formal compositions, each piece containing arrangements of mixed flowers tied with ribbons. The compositions were coloured by Dixon himself with the help of some young artists whom he employed from the Dublin Society Schools, many of whom went on to become miniature painters. Variations in style were inevitable as these were hand-coloured watercolours. Some of the assistants can be identified because the artists initialed the plates. The pictures were sold inserted in decorative gold, japanned and peartree frames with shaped glass.

Samuel Dixon had a varied career. He trained at the Dublin Society Schools, after which he opened a picture shop in Capel Street, selling all kinds of art materials and dealing in pictures. It was during these years that he issued his sets of watercolours. He subsequently spent time abroad (1756-58), ran a linen-printing industry in Leixlip, Co. Kildare, and owned a picture shop in London up to 1768. He died the following year in Dublin.

George Barret (1732-84)

POWERSCOURT WATERFALL, CO. WICKLOW c.1760

Oil on canvas,
100 x 127 cm
NGI NO. 174

GEORGE BARRET was born in the Liberties in Dublin. He learned to draw under Robert West, later headmaster at the Dublin Society Schools. It was Edmund Burke, the noted philosopher, orator and writer, who influenced him to paint landscapes showing real places. Barret must have been aware of Burke's ideas on the sublime and the beautiful, which were published some years later. Burke held that what was sublime in nature was vast, awesome, terrible and uncontrollable, whereas the beautiful was denoted by small-ness, tranquillity, gentleness and sweetness. Burke may have introduced the artist to Lord Powerscourt, who owned a splendid demesne some forty kilometres south of Dublin, at Enniskerry, Co. Wicklow, with a magnificent house designed by the German architect Richard Cassels. Successive Viscounts Powerscourt added to the beauty of the property and welcomed visitors, especially artists. Barret spent several years painting at the Powerscourt estate. This portrayal of *Powerscourt Waterfall* is one of a number of pictures by him featuring the famous cascade with its impressive falls of 116 metres. Barret's composition represents the sublime in nature, with the tiny figure-group in the foreground contrasting with the huge trees (themselves planted to enhance the scene), the vast wooded landscape, the high cliffs and the powerful waterfall. The artist responds fully to Burke's observations about nature, choosing to depict the scene in mid summer, with heavily leaved trees, verdant cliffs, and an Italianate golden light of evening reflected on the foaming torrent of water.

Barret moved to London in 1763, bringing with him a number of his landscapes. He showed the paintings at exhibitions in the city, and had no problems finding buyers and gaining rapid acclaim. Numerous commissions followed, resulting in a very successful practice painting landscape views and romantic scenery throughout England, Scotland, Wales and the Isle of Wight. Such was his success that his annual income was sometimes as much as two thousand pounds, an enormous figure at a time when a contemporary of his, the English artist Richard Wilson, was barely able to sustain himself by his art. Barret was a founder member of the Royal Academy in London and regularly showed at its exhibitions. Bad management of his financial affairs led him almost to bankruptcy. His friend Edmund Burke helped him in 1782 to obtain the post of master painter to Chelsea Hospital. When Barret died in 1784, he left his family impoverished. However, in recognition of his contribution to their institution, the Royal Academy granted the family a modest pension.

Patrick Cunningham (fl.1750-74)

JONATHAN SWIFT (1667-1745), SATIRIST AND DEAN OF ST PATRICK'S CATHEDRAL, DUBLIN c.1766

Marble,
37 cm ht.
NGI NO. 8026

JONATHAN SWIFT was the most celebrated dean of St Patrick's Cathedral, Dublin, but he is equally famous as a poet, satirist and political writer. Born in Dublin, the son of an English-born lawyer, Swift became vicar of Kilroot, Co. Antrim, in 1695/6. The next appointment was at Laracor, Co. Meath, in 1700. His publication, *A Tale of a Tub* (1704), a religious allegory, lampooned Catholicism and Non-conformism. In 1707 Swift returned to England to negotiate financial concessions for the Church of Ireland. He was involved in Tory politics and wrote highly effective propaganda, particularly against the continuation of war with France. Swift's efforts won him appointment as Dean of St Patrick's Cathedral in Dublin (1713), but not the English bishopric that he had hoped for. The exclusion of the Tories from power after 1714 forced him back to Ireland. During the 1720s he became a fierce controversialist on Irish issues, notably advocating, by means of pamphlets, a boycott of English goods. Other pamphlets attacked English misgovernment of Ireland and exploitative and absentee landlordism. His satirical *A Modest Proposal* (1792), which argued that Ireland could escape from poverty by raising children for food, is his personal indictment of England's oppression of Ireland. *Gulliver's Travels* (1726) is a more broadly based satire on contemporary politics, religion and literature.

Patrick Cunningham was master of the realistic manner, as is evident from this bust of Swift executed about 1766. The marble head and neck shows a middle-aged man, with short curly hair, looking to the side. What is striking about this work is how Swift's character and personality are so succinctly captured, despite the fact that it is a posthumous work. The expression on his small, full mouth is one of ironic amusement. His eyes, alert beneath the large bushy eyebrows, denote a sharp observer of the human condition. There are no clothes or wig to distract the eye. The success of the carved portrait rests on its convincing physical likeness and its sense of the man. This is a hallmark of the sculptor Patrick Cunningham. Cunningham trained at the Dublin Society Schools and in the studio of John Van Nost the Younger (d.1780), who came to Ireland from Holland and who introduced the fashion for portrait busts into this country. He was recognised among his contemporaries primarily as a wax modeller, a miniature form of sculpture, and his exhibits at the Society of Artists in Ireland, while including busts in terracotta and marble, were in the main portraits modelled in coloured wax.

Joseph Blackburn (fl.1752-78)

PORTRAIT OF A YOUNG GIRL HOLDING A DUBLIN LOTTERY TICKET 1767

Oil on canvas,
76 x 63 cm
NGI NO. 4456

LITTLE IS KNOWN about the artist Joseph Blackburn, who came to prominence in America but was probably trained in London. He is first recorded in Bermuda in 1752/3. He subsequently painted in Massachusetts and New Hampshire and is believed to have been on a visit to Dublin in the 1760-67 period, when funds were being raised for the new Exchange project. This painting, executed in 1767, and inspired by the new Exchange, depicts a little girl, dressed in a pink and white dress, with pretty red pumps, complete with a decorative floral wreath in her hair. Holding aloft a large ticket in her hand, she invites the viewer to read what is inscribed on it. It reads:

No. 45 662 Dublin Anno 1767

Fifty Days after the drawing of State Lottery
For 1767 is finished the BEARER hereof
Will be entitled to y:e Prize arising
to y:e same Number in...said lottery pursuant
to y:e Scheme Published by the
Merchants for building a NEW
EXCHANGE on Cork Hill...Parliament Street
Exd By Order
J Grant....Transfer

Lotteries have been in existence since the fifteenth century, and the first actual game of Lotto was played with such success in Genoa that it was taken over by the State, spread throughout the country and then through Europe. Lotteries were very popular in eighteenth-century Dublin, and Capel and Grafton Streets were the main areas for the ticket offices. They became such a rage (with some beginning and ending the same day) that laws were passed to put a stop to the throngs of people who visited the offices, often waiting long hours for results. The ticket in the painting concerns the need to raise money for the building of a new Exchange to replace the previous one, then in a ruinous state, which was located on Skinner's Row, opposite Christ Church Cathedral. Partly with money from lotteries, the merchants purchased a site on Cork Hill for £13,500 and raised £40,000 for the building. It would later become the City Hall. When sufficient funds had been raised, sixty-one designs were submitted to a competition in 1768. Thomas Cooley came first, ahead even of James Gandon, the architect responsible for some of the finest buildings in Dublin in the eighteenth century. The lord lieutenant, Lord Townsend, laid the foundation stone on 2 August 1769, and the New Merchants' Exchange (soon to be renamed the Royal Exchange) was complete by 1779.

Nathaniel Hone the Elder (1718-84)

THE PIPING BOY, 1769

Oil on canvas,
36 x 31 cm
NGI NO. 440

AT THE AGE of ten, John Camillus Hone (1759-1836), one of several children of the artist Nathaniel Hone, had his portrait painted by his father, whose depiction of another son, *Horace Hone Sketching* (1766), is also in the National Gallery's Collection. *The Piping Boy*, inscribed 'N. Hone 1769', was exhibited at the Royal Academy in 1769, where it was one of the paintings which excited the greatest admiration of the critic Northcote (*Memoirs of Sir Joshua Reynolds*, 1813). It was later engraved by W. Baillie in 1771. Nathaniel Hone was born in Dublin in 1718, the son of a merchant from Wood Quay whose family is thought to have emigrated from Holland in the seventeenth century. He spent the early part of his career, from about 1740 onwards, as an enamelist and miniaturist working in watercolour on ivory. In 1742 he was in York, where he married, after which he settled in London. Hone established his reputation in London painting life-size oils. After Zincke's retirement in 1752, he succeeded him as the foremost enamel portrait painter in miniature, signing himself 'NH'. The artist preferred Dutch realism to the influence of Italian art, even though this picture is inspired by a work by Giorgione now in Hampton Court, London. Hone treats the portrait in a Dutch style, using strong contrasts of light and shade, and a soft outline demarking the features and clothing of the child. Fine and detailed brushwork has been employed in the painting of the hair and fur jacket. The dark, thoughtful eyes suggest that the boy is wrapped up in the music he is playing. This is a sensitive portrait of Camillus Hone by an obviously devoted father.

The painting is considered to be a realistic depiction of the young boy and not an idealised portrait. The concept of childhood as a distinct and precious state, and the child as innocent rather than merely ignorant, took conscious shape in the eighteenth century. It became almost universal under the impact of Rousseau and the Romantic poets. It was an era when people began to see childhood, not as a preparation for something else, but as a separate stage, often the best stage in life. Paintings such as *The Piping Boy* reflect this new parental tenderness for children. According to Strickland's *Dictionary of Irish Artists*, published in 1913, Hone was deeply attached to his large family, who feature prominently in his paintings, and he mentioned several in his diaries: Nathaniel, Horace (1756-1825) and John Camillus (1759-1836), both of whom went on to become miniature portrait painters, Samuel and Apelles, Lydia, Amelia, Mary, Sophia and Henrietta. This type of children's portraiture became a significant part of the artist's oeuvre. While it is an informal studio painting, the artist manages to achieve a level of immediacy and freshness without intruding on the boy's innocent pursuit. It is one of Hone's most accomplished portraits.

Francis Robert West (c.1749-1809)

PORTRAIT OF A GENTLEMAN IN A GREY COAT 1772

Charcoal and pastel
on paper,
47.4 x 38 cm
NGI NO. 3834

*P*ortrait of a Gentleman in a Grey Coat was signed and dated by West in 1772. It is one of four large oval portraits, two of which are dated 1772. They are all executed in charcoal and pastel on paper. There is enough similarity in the shape of the face and features, particularly the round-shaped eyes, to suggest that the unidentified sitters may have been members of the same family. The Dublin Society Drawing Schools excelled at teaching in the medium of pastel, and West's *Portrait of a Gentleman in a Grey Coat* is a perfect example of the work of this generation of skilled pastellists.

Francis Robert West was the son of Robert West, who was one of the founders (along with Samuel Madden and Thomas Prior) and first master of the Dublin Society Schools. Very little is known about Robert West. He was born in Waterford and educated in France, and he reputedly trained in Paris under Boucher, where he would have been taught to use chalk and pastel. It was in the late 1730s that West opened his private drawing school in Dublin. Although Isaac Weld, in his account in *Observations on the Royal Dublin Society and Its Existing Institutions in the Year 1831* (Dublin 1831), indicates that the date of the private drawing school's change of status into the Royal Dublin Society's Drawing School is somewhat vague, according to Strickland, Madden and Prior arranged with West around 1744 that he would instruct twelve boys. The Dublin Society Drawing School was located in West's George's Lane premises and it appears that the intention was to found a fine art school together with a trade school. During this period the Drawing Schools produced a generation of skilled pastellists, who absorbed French influences through the headmaster. Although Robert West was regarded as a superb draughtsman, regrettably no drawing of his survives. The Schools were hugely successful in their lifetime and were taken over by the Government in 1849. In 1877 they were renamed the Metropolitan School of Art, now the National College of Art and Design.

Francis Robert West was taught by his father to draw in crayon and pastel. Other artists who may have been at the Schools at the same time include Robert Healy (1743-71) and Thomas Hickey (1741-1824). W.B. Sarsfield Taylor suggests that West may have spent some time at the French Academy of Arts (*The Origin, Progress, and Present Condition of the Fine Arts in Great Britain and Ireland*, London 1841). West is recorded as having exhibited in Dublin with the Society of Artists in Ireland between 1770 and 1801, showing a variety of works, including religious subjects, portraits, mythological themes, historical drawings and 'portraits in conversation'. Francis Robert West succeeded his father in 1771 in the mastership of the Dublin Society Drawing Schools.

Thomas Roberts (1748-78)

LUCAN HOUSE AND DEMESNE, CO. DUBLIN c.1772

Oil on canvas,
60.5 x 100 cm
NGI NO. 4463

THOMAS ROBERTS was the son of the noted Waterford architect, John Roberts, who designed the Catholic and Church of Ireland cathedrals and some fine mansions in the city. After a basic education, Roberts attended the Dublin Society Drawing Schools under the landscape painter James Mannin. It was in his first year, 1763, that he won a prize at the School of Landscape and Ornament. Following his training, he became apprenticed to George Mullins, an accomplished landscape painter who also kept an ale house in the Temple Bar area of Dublin. From 1766 to 1777 Roberts exhibited at the Society of Artists and was renowned for his topographical views. His *Ideal Landscape* in the National Gallery's collection, based on a classically inspired Claudian landscape model, but also reflecting some Dutch influence, is one of the most accomplished eighteenth-century pictures of the period, affirming his position as one of Ireland's foremost landscape artists.

While Thomas Roberts was a fine figure painter, it was, however, for his topographical paintings that he became justifiably renowned. Many leading eighteenth-century Italian view painters, such as Canaletto and Bellotto, catered for the wealthy classes, who purchased their views on the 'grand tour' of Italy. Because of the realism shown in Roberts' depiction of houses and their estates, such as in *Lucan House and Demesne*, it is correct to describe him as a view painter. In this view we find the artist painting the attractive lower reaches of the river Liffey. There is also a measure of idealisation in the Italian manner, particularly in the handling of the light. The National Gallery is fortunate in having a set of four high-quality views of Lucan house and parts of the estate by this artist. The view illustrated here, showing old Lucan House, is historically very important and is dated to 1772, when the owner, Agmondisham Vesey, was designing his new house. In the late twelfth century a castle was built here, later owned by the earls of Kildare. By 1564 it belonged to the Sarsfield family, passing to Patrick Sarsfield, who in 1691 was created Earl of Lucan by King James II. Sarsfield's niece married Agmondisham Vesey and his eldest son built the Palladian house which still stands and is the residence of the Italian ambassador to Ireland. The picture shows old Lucan house and the tiny village of Lucan from the banks of the river Liffey on the road to Dublin. In the bottom corner a group of men are seen quarrying stone, and apart from lending scale to the landscape, the figures take on a life of their own. Roberts has depicted them with deft, quick brushstrokes, which lend an air of life and energy to the composition. Unfortunately the artist's short life came to an end in 1778 while he was visiting Lisbon, a visit he had undertaken for the benefit of his health.

Nathaniel Hone the Elder (1718-84)

THE CONJUROR 1775

Oil on canvas,
145 x 173 cm
NGI NO. 1790

*T*he Conjuror, Nathaniel Hone's best-known painting, caused controversy when it was first exhibited in 1775 at the Royal Academy in London. The picture illustrates a magician who 'conjures up' a painting by borrowing from prints of works by the old masters. The president of the Royal Academy, Sir Joshua Reynolds, who had recently given a lecture about the importance of copying the works of the great masters, quickly realised that this was an attack on himself. The implication was that Reynolds had relied heavily on these images to create his own paintings. Hone did not believe in borrowing from the old masters and therefore his picture slighted Reynolds. The full title of the picture is: *The Pictorial Conjuror, Displaying the Whole Art of Optical Deception*, and after a brief showing at the Academy its removal was requested.

In addition to attacking Reynolds' artistic practice, Hone was also accused of depicting a nude figure, allegedly the well-known female artist Angelica Kaufmann, who was a friend of Reynolds. Hone denied the accusation and reluctantly agreed to paint over the nude, replacing it with a scene of artists around a table, with St Paul's Cathedral in the background. There were also other dimensions to the story. There was the persistent rumour that Kaufmann and Reynolds were involved in a relationship. The model for the old man was George White, frequently employed by Reynolds, while the young girl leaning on the conjuror's knee is reputed to have been based on an engraving after Angelica Kaufmann. The pose is evocative of the style of Reynolds. In this picture the owl on the right is included as a symbol of folly, in keeping with Northern European tradition, whereas in Graeco-Roman tradition it alluded to wisdom. Hone was furious with the outcome and withdrew from the Royal Academy. Without delay he organised a display of his work, the first one-man show ever held in the British Isles.

Nathaniel Hone the Elder was born in Dublin (there is no record of his training), before going to London, where he established a successful career as a fashionable portrait and subject painter. One of the finest portrait painters Ireland has ever produced, Hone was also a superb painter of children. In 1768 he became a foundation member of the Royal Academy, but his fiery temper brought him into conflict with the establishment, especially over this painting. Although *The Conjuror* was designed as a satire on a famous painter, Reynolds, it is a beautifully executed painting. Hone's refusal to follow academic rules was to provide a role model in later years for artists of the Romantic movement.

James Barry (1741-1806)

THE DEATH OF ADONIS, c.1775

Oil on canvas,
100 x 126 cm
NGI NO. 1393

JAMES BARRY was a tradesman's son from Cork, who came to Dublin to pursue art training. His ambition was to be a great history painter, because history painting was considered the most important branch of painting by academic theorists of the day. He became interested in Edmund Burke's theories of the sublime and beautiful, and it was Burke who arranged his trip to London and financed his stay in Paris and Rome. Back in London in 1771 his talent brought him immediate recognition as a significant painter of history subjects. Barry believed that the purpose of art was to instruct and enrich, and he used his skills to convey an heroic vision, using subjects from history and mythology. The grandeur of his vision brought him fame but his difficult and troublesome personality created unhappiness. He died in poverty, a proud and isolated man, refusing to lower his standards by painting fashionable and lucrative portraits.

Barry depicted the story 'The Death of Adonis' from Ovid's *Metamorphoses*, as it enabled him to expand into the more lyrical aspects of classical subject matter. The story relates how Venus fell in love with Adonis, but unfortunately Adonis was fatally gored by a wild boar which he had wounded while hunting. The picture shows Venus mourning her lover, as she tenderly rests his head on her knees. One cupid vainly feels Adonis' pulse, while a second stands close by, weeping. In the background, two greyhounds echo the sorrowful mood as they ceaselessly whimper and cry. To the right, Venus' chariot is visible, decorated with a scene of her birth. Two doves can be seen, representing love, but also the soul, and they are harnessed to the chariot in readiness to travel through the skies. The dark boar can be observed in the distance, exiting from the scene. This is a most accomplished work in which Barry attempts to convey the sweet sadness of the story. Adonis was an intrepid hunter, and the sight of his tiny horn and slender spear lying useless beside his body emphasise the fatality of the scene. The small scale of the figures, enclosed within a beautiful landscape, reinforces the sentimental mood and drama of the story. Barry employs an economy of carefully chosen motifs, which enhance the melancholic mood and evoke the sympathy of the viewer.

Francis Wheatley (1747-1801)

THE DUBLIN VOLUNTEERS IN COLLEGE GREEN, 4 NOVEMBER 1779

Oil on canvas,
175 x 323 cm
NGI NO. 125

WHEATLEY WAS a London-born artist, whose arrival in Ireland in 1779 coincided with the rise of the Irish Volunteers. This was a military body formed in 1778/9 to provide protection against a feared French invasion, at a time when the number of English troops was being reduced. At first its members were predominantly Protestant, but soon Catholics were permitted to join. The Volunteers, who were well supported by the gentry and nobility, promoted an independent Irish parliament, seeking repeal of all restrictions on Irish trade. The purpose of Wheatley's trip to Ireland was to flee his creditors. He arrived in the country with the wife of a fellow artist. During his four years in Ireland he painted some of his finest works, including *The Dublin Volunteers in College Green*, a unique record of an important historical event. Wheatley's prolific output included portraits, landscapes, conversation pieces and some historic works. His term in Ireland came to an abrupt end when he found himself in debt and the nature of his relationship with the artist's wife was discovered. This was not acceptable in eighteenth-century Dublin society and he was obliged to return to England in 1783.

Before the Act of Union in 1800, Henry Grattan dominated Irish politics. One of his main arguments was that restrictive trade laws had to go and that the Irish parliament be made independent. This was a time of heightened political activity. Wheatley was present in Dublin to record the nine hundred Dublin Volunteers parading on 4 November 1779 in College Green to celebrate the birthday of William III, in front of his statue. The Volunteers are shown wearing a blue uniform with a red collar, made from Irish fabric and paid for by their leaders. Each Volunteer group had its own distinguishing insignia. The colourful ceremony and uniformed troops contributed to the excitement of the occasion. Key figures included Luke Gardiner, a colonel of the Volunteers, and the Duke of Leinster, standing in the centre of the composition, with Sir Edward Newenham on the left. Depicted under a green parasol on the third building from the left is Princess Daschkaw, a lady of honour to the Empress Catherine the Great of Russia. In the centre of the picture Wheatley shows the twin-pedimented porticos of the Houses of Parliament, designed by Sir Edward Lovett Pearce. The artist also portrays Trinity College accurately, showing a large Italianate dome rising from Front Square, by the Palladian architect Richard Castle. It had to be dismantled in 1791 due to fears of its instability. The show of strength displayed by the Irish Volunteers that day was one of the reasons why the English parliament repealed the restrictive trade laws.

Jonathan Fisher (fl.1763-1809)

A VIEW OF THE LOWER LAKE, KILLARNEY 1780s

Oil on canvas,
39.8 x 52 cm
NGI NO. 1797

THIS PAINTING, a fine example of a work by Jonathan Fisher, is almost certainly the basis for one of a series of aquatints published in Dublin in 1789 depicting twenty views of the Killarney area. In the central area of the scene is the lake, a popular tourist haunt both then and now. It is divided into two by a grassy inlet. The immense stretch of water reaches back into the far distance, from where a range of mountains marks the horizon. The foreground of the picture depicts some clumps of rocks and a tall thin tree is silhouetted against a vast expanse of sky. The scene appears to have been recorded on a tranquil summer's day. Nothing seems to stir. Dotted on the horizon to the right are some houses, the only indication of human habitation. Although the scene is of a named place, the artist has carefully constructed and framed his composition to create a sweeping sense of distance, and the viewer is encouraged to forget that what is painted is in fact on a flat canvas. It is a delightful view, evocative of a still, warm summer's evening, when nature appears at its most calm and beautiful.

Unusual for an Irish artist working in the late eighteenth century, Jonathan Fisher had been a successful woollen draper in the Liberties of Dublin before becoming an artist. It is believed that he received his training in London. In 1763, when he was living in Dublin, he was awarded a premium of ten guineas for a landscape by the Dublin Society. He was a regular contributor to various exhibitions until 1801. From 1788 to his death he held the post of supervisor of stamps in the Stamp Office, Eustace Street, Dublin. Fisher concentrated on views of actual scenery rather than ideal views, and many of these were engraved from his paintings. He contributed to a growing preference among artists in the mid eighteenth century for 'unspoilt' landscape and he was one of the first to popularise the romantic scenery of Kerry. In 1770 he published six large views of Killarney, which were engraved by various artists – views of Carlingford in 1772, and sixty plates of the scenery of Ireland from 1796.

Horace Hone (c.1756-1825)

MRS SARAH SIDDONS (1755-1831), ACTRESS 1784

Watercolour on
ivory,
9.2 x 7.6 cm
NGI NO. 7318

THE ENGLISH ACTRESS Sarah Siddons first came to Ireland in the summer of 1783, encouraged by the success of her brother, John Philip Kemble, who had been acting in Dublin since November 1781. Her first performance was at the Smock Alley Theatre, on 21 June. A contemporary account tells of how the theatre was packed with people, all anxious to see this already famous actress. Her dramatic abilities were clearly convincing because it is recorded how emotionally affected the audience was by her performance. Much too was made of her physical beauty and her graceful carriage. Sarah Siddons' private account of her stay in Dublin is not uncritical. In a letter she stated that Dublin was dirty and noisy. She also professed to not liking its inhabitants. Yet she acknowledged that she had earned a thousand pounds for her work that summer. She concluded that while she felt obliged to the citizens of Dublin because they certainly appreciated her acting abilities, she could not love them!

The miniature is dated 1784 and was executed during Siddons' second stay in the city, two years after Hone had settled in Dublin. It depicts her, head and shoulders, in three-quarter profile. She is wearing a fashionable open-necked dress of the period. Her hair, swept loosely back, curls prettily at the nape of her neck. Her features are regular in a classical way and the perfectly shaped eyebrows and deep, dark eyes indicate that the actress was indeed a beauty of her day. The expression on her face is wistful and she seems deep in thought; so much so that the viewer has the impression that she is unaware of the artist sketching her. The medium used is watercolour and the delicacy of the brushwork points to a very skilled hand.

Horace Hone was the second son of the artist Nathaniel Hone the Elder. He was taught miniature painting by his father and attended the Royal Academy School in London. He painted miniature portraits in watercolour and enamel, exhibiting these at the Royal Academy, London, over a long period, starting in 1772. Hone settled in Dublin in 1782 and worked in Ireland, receiving ample patronage until 1804, when he returned to London. Hone was appointed miniature painter to the Prince of Wales in 1795. He spent the year 1804 in Bath, following which he returned to London to be close to his fashionable clients. The small size of Hone's miniatures gradually increased during his time in Ireland, allowing for the creation of larger portraits. The National Gallery of Ireland has a dozen miniature portraits by him. These include a portrayal of James Gandon, architect of the Custom House and Four Courts buildings in Dublin. Horace Hone was one of a group of distinguished miniaturists, including Adam Buck and Sampson Towgood Roch, that established Dublin as a centre of miniature painting in the mid eighteenth century.

Thomas Hickey (1741-1824)

AN INDIAN LADY 1787

Oil on canvas,
102 x 127 cm
NGI NO. 1390

IT IS NOT SURPRISING to find that the painter of this portrait, Thomas Hickey, led an exciting and adventurous life. Hickey, who was born in Dublin in 1741, trained at the Dublin Society Schools (1753-56) winning several prizes, from where he emerged a competent and versatile portraitist. The lack of opportunity to advance his career in Ireland forced him to emigrate. He spent six years studying in Italy in the 1760s, and after a period in Dublin, London and Bath, he appears to have decided to try his fortune further afield in the East. On 27 July 1780 he left Portsmouth in a convoy of five East Indiamen sailing for India. The ship on which he was travelling was captured on 9 August by French and Spanish fleets. Hickey was put ashore at Cadiz and given permission to return to England. However, he remained in Portugal, where he found good patrons among the British community, as a result of which he did not leave for India until late 1783. Hickey spent the years 1784-1824 in India. In 1792 he returned to London, with one trip home in 1796. The artist returned to India in 1798, where he remained for the rest of his life.

When he first arrived in Calcutta in 1784, Hickey spent seven years executing portraits of the expatriot British community. He was befriended by William Hickey (no relation of the artist), an attorney and diarist, who became his patron. *An Indian Lady* is one of the most successful pictures of Hickey's Calcutta period, the subject of which is thought to be Jemandee, the mistress of William Hickey. Jemandee is portrayed as being totally passive, resting against cushions on a colonnaded veranda, a popular feature of European homes in Calcutta, lost in her own thoughts, looking beyond into the distance. The picture reveals assured brushwork in the painting of the figure and exotic clothing, with the background depicted in a more sketchy manner to create the effect of the humid, hazy atmosphere of India. The most striking feature of this portrait is the evocative and haunting presence of the Indian girl.

Hugh Douglas Hamilton (c.1739-1808)

FREDERICK HERVEY, BISHOP OF DERRY AND FOURTH EARL OF BRISTOL (1730-1803) WITH HIS GRANDDAUGHTER LADY CAROLINE CRICHTON (1779-1856), IN THE GARDENS OF THE VILLA BORGHESE, ROME, c.1790

Oil on canvas,
230 x 199 cm
NGI NO. 4350

HUGH DOUGLAS HAMILTON was the most successful of the many Irish artists working in Rome during the second half of the eighteenth century. He had achieved fame as a portrait painter of small ovals in crayon and pencil and later in oils, in Ireland and in England, before going to Rome in 1782. During his time there, Hamilton worked hard to develop his full potential within a circle which included the Irish painter Henry Tresham, the English sculptor John Flaxman and the Italian neo-classical sculptor Antonio Canova. Canova, who was a close friend of the artist, is represented in the National Gallery's collection by a superb figure of an Amorino or Cupid, commissioned by the La Touche family, who were Dublin Bankers. Hamilton was successful at finding patrons among the Grand Tourists – those Irish and English aristocrats who sought to further their education and absorb the cultural aspects of foreign travel by undertaking a trip to the Continent, with Rome as its climax.

The Earl-Bishop was a frequent traveller, distinguished clergyman and patron of the arts. He was bishop of the richest diocese of the Church of Ireland and in order to travel he delegated his duties. For an Englishman who held high office in Ireland, he was unusual in being sympathetic to the idea of Catholic Emancipation, and he built several Catholic churches in his diocese. He was also opposed to the Act of Union. A regular visitor to Rome, the Earl-Bishop was deeply involved in artistic circles. He commissioned Hamilton to do several works. Hamilton, in common with other artists of the time, managed a regular practice of portrait painting, while also doing history painting based on the study of classical history and mythology. Lady Caroline Crichton accompanied her mother Lady Erne to Rome in 1785 and remained travelling in Italy until 1790. In Hamilton's portrait, the Earl-Bishop is shown in the idyllic gardens of the Villa Borghese in Rome. Lady Caroline has put down her drawing portfolio to point out a relief of the 'Seasons' on the Altar of the Twelve Gods. The altar, a piece of antique Roman carving which was later acquired by Napoleon, is now housed in the Louvre. The landscape in the background shows a beautifully painted view of the park, with the recently completed Temple of Aesculapius situated beside the tree-lined lake, reflecting the revival of interest in the art of ancient Rome in this period.

Attributed to Nathaniel Grogan (c.1740-1807)

A LANDSCAPE AT TIVOLI, CORK, WITH BOATS 1790s

Oil on canvas,
94 x 166 cm
NGI NO. 4074

The view illustrated possibly shows the estuary of the river Lee, looking up towards the city of Cork. To the left of the foreground is a group of boats, including a rowing boat in which are seated several passengers. Five of them are in conversation with each other. The remaining passengers are more intent on watching what is happening on the river. In the centre a single-masted fishing smack can be seen. It is almost certainly a pleasure craft. The pall of rising smoke indicates an explosion, which may be the midday gun but could also be a signal-to-shore of some kind. A small boat is close by. On the north bank of the river are two Gothic follies and along the pathway are people with horses, perhaps a forge, and a horse-drawn carriage with passengers. A grand house is strikingly located on a height overlooking the river. In the far distance the city itself can be seen through a warm haze.

In style, the work is dependent on Dutch maritime art. The scene is painted in muted tones of soft brown and green, while the sky behind is brilliantly illuminated. The artist creates a convincing sense of place in his careful attention to the different elements which make up the landscape and his record of the busy life on the river. But the depiction may not be quite as accurate as it looks. It is very likely that the painter, in the manner of landscape artists of the time, sketched the area around Tivoli first on the spot and then worked up the final canvas in his studio.

A largely self-taught artist, Grogan was born in Cork. Before pursuing a career in art, he was apprenticed to his father, a turner and block-maker. He longed to be an artist, but on receiving no encouragement from his family he enlisted in the army. His early career in the army included a visit to America. He returned to Cork and made an adequate living as an artist, painting and giving drawing lessons. He was also employed to decorate Vernon Mount, where he depicted Minerva and other classical figures. Grogan is best remembered for his genre scenes, which are so informative about the life and surroundings of ordinary people at this time. In this painting, landscape and genre successfully merge to produce a convincing vignette of life in the Cork countryside in the eighteenth century.

Hugh Douglas Hamilton (c.1739-1808)

WILLIAM MILLBANK IN FRONT OF THE TEMPLE OF VESPASIAN 1791

Pastel on paper,
95 x 67 cm
NGI NO. 7731

HAMILTON IS AN EXAMPLE of an Irish artist whose time in Rome during the later eighteenth century provided him with a wide-ranging education and experience, and allowed him pit his talents against contemporary artists from all over Europe. Trained initially in the Dublin Society Schools, he specialised in small oval portraits in crayon and pastel, of uniform size, exhibiting them at the Society of Artists in Dublin, before moving to London. He abandoned a highly successful portrait practice in London in order to study history painting in Italy. He was there between 1779 and 1782, spending time in Rome, Florence, Naples and Venice. Following his return to Ireland in 1792, Hamilton had a successful career as a portraitist but, much to his disappointment, found little interest in his history pictures. He did not manage to revisit Italy before he died, in 1808, in Dublin.

One of the artist's late Roman sitters was William Millbank (1768-1802), who is depicted against a temple in the Roman Forum. Dressed in the typical clothing of a young man on the Grand Tour, Millbank commissioned his portrait to commemorate the visit. The Grand Tour, considered to be an essential part of a gentleman's education, involved a trip to the Continent, with Rome as the climax. It was undertaken by Irish and English aristocrats who wished to improve their European languages, view the splendours of Rome, absorb the refinement acquired by foreign travel, and generally enjoy themselves. Many of these tourists collected works of art and antiquities for their estates, like the Leesons and La Touches, thereby spreading the taste in Ireland for Italian culture. Millbank, aged twenty-four, is shown against the Temple of Vespasian on the Palatine Hill, which was located at the west end of the Roman Forum. During nineteenth-century excavations, the temple was fully uncovered, down to its foundations.

Few full-length pastel portraits are known to have been executed by Hamilton before he went to Italy, but after his arrival in Rome he used this portrait-type more frequently. In common with other eighteenth-century neo-classical artists, Hamilton was fascinated with Roman art arising from the recent archaeological excavations. This ambitious composition shows the influence of fashionable Grand Tour portraitists, such as Pompei Batoni. It is a most accomplished portrait; the pastel has been executed in a smooth, soft style, with the figure finely drawn and posed realistically within his surroundings.

James Malton (c.1760-1803)

THE CUSTOM HOUSE, DUBLIN 1793

Ink and watercolour
on paper,
53.6 x 77 cm
NGI NO. 2705

THE CUSTOM HOUSE is perhaps the best-known building in Dublin. It was the first of James Gandon's designs in the development of Georgian Dublin and replaced the old Custom House which had been located further up river at Essex Quay. Gandon had already made a name for himself in London when, in 1781, he accepted an invitation to come to Dublin. He appears to have encountered opposition about this project almost from the start. There were those who believed that their vested interests would not be served by the changed location of the new building, which would shift the existing centre of commerce. The daring way in which he tackled the problem of building the foundations on reclaimed slob-land also created controversy. He decided to use a base of timber, with brick and granite, instead of simple piling.

Located on the north bank of the river Liffey, the Custom House presents an imposing façade. Its long horizontals perfectly echo the elongated shape of the river. It is 114 metres (375 feet) long and 62 metres (205 feet) deep. The central projection is joined to the end pavilions by arcades, each with seven arches. All the columns along the building's front incorporate harps in their capitals. A graceful copper dome with four pedimented clocks, surmounted by the figure of Commerce, complete the design. The building contains much sculpture: swags, trophies, allegorical figures and keystones of Irish river gods. The team of sculptors was led by Edward Smyth, who often collaborated with James Gandon, the architect.

Malton was born into a family associated with recording architecture. He is thought to have worked in the office of James Gandon but later turned against him. This water-colour, dating from 1793, is one of twenty-five views of Dublin, engraved in aquatint, a process for producing tone etchings that resemble watercolour drawings in quality. They were issued individually from 1792 to 1799, at which date they appeared bound with a commentary under the title *A Picturesque and Descriptive View of the City of Dublin*. Malton's fame rests largely on his twenty-five views of the city. This book is still popular today and copies of Malton's prints are highly sought after among art collectors.

William Ashford (1746-1824)

THE OPENING OF THE RINGSEND DOCKS, DUBLIN 1796

Oil on canvas,
74 x 95 cm
NGI NO. 4614

IN THIS VIEW, Lord Camden, the lord lieutenant, watched by a crowd of over 150,000, opens the Grand Canal Docks at Ringsend on 23 April 1796, St George's Day. During the eighteenth century, Ringsend served as the port to Dublin. Towards the end of the century considerable work was done to improve the harbour; it was greatly enlarged and linked to the Grand Canal. This involved building lock gates from the river Liffey in 1790, and the following year a basin and docks were completed. Lord Camden entered the docks on a yacht, and after hoisting the Royal Standard, was rowed ashore. The canopied boat in the centre of the scene was the one used by Lord Camden. About twenty other vessels also entered the docks, forming a grand parade, accompanied by decorated barges and pleasure boats.

In the picture there is a small opening among the crowd of figures on the quayside, where Lord Camden can be seen conferring a knighthood on John Macartney, Chairman of the Court of Directors of the Grand Canal Company. The conferring was followed by a great breakfast for about a thousand in the tents shown in the background. It was a splendid occasion and contemporary accounts estimated that hundreds of thousands of spectators viewed the event. This superb view, signed and dated 1796, and later purchased by the architect Francis Johnston, represents a genuine attempt by the artist to capture an important historical event.

William Ashford was born in Birmingham in 1746. Following his education, he came to Ireland in 1764, having obtained a minor post in the Ordnance office, which he held until 1788. By 1767 he was exhibiting flower pieces. Ashford quickly developed into a highly accomplished classical landscape painter, very much in demand to record views of houses and their estates. He was a regular contributor to the Society of Artists' exhibitions, earned a sizable income and was also a noted collector. In 1792 his friend James Gandon designed a villa for him in Sandymount in Dublin, where he lived for the remainder of his life. Ashford was an extremely highly regarded painter in Ireland. His reputation was such that, even after his retirement, he was invited in 1823 to become the first President of the Royal Hibernian Academy. This was a great honour for a landscape painter, although he didn't survive to see the first exhibition in 1826.

Thomas Sautelle Roberts (1760-1826)

A LANDSCAPE c.1800

Oil on canvas,
57 x 83 cm
NGI NO. 848

THOMAS SAUTELLE ROBERTS was the younger brother of the renowned eighteenth-century landscape painter, Thomas Roberts. In 1777 he attended the Dublin Society Architectural Drawing Schools and was apprenticed for a time to Thomas Ivory, the neo-classical architect, before deciding to become a painter. Sautelle was only eighteen when his elder brother died in 1778, after which he took Thomas as his first name. Before 1800 his preferred medium was watercolour and he held a one-man show of his watercolours in 1801 in Dublin. While his early oil paintings are similar in style to those of his brother, he had a tendency to use stronger lighting, and in his later works he displayed a greater interest in rugged scenery. Roberts began exhibiting Irish and English views in 1789 at the Royal Academy, continuing to do so up to 1811, and at the British Institution from 1807 to 1818. He was also known for his depictions of horses and dogs. His pictures of architectural subjects were much admired, although none of these survive. Twelve aquatints of Irish scenery, part of an uncompleted project, were published between 1795 and 1799 under the title *Illustrations of the Chief Cities, Rivers, Ruins and Picturesque Scenery of the Kingdom of Ireland.* These aquatints are some of the most valued eighteenth-century prints in the National Gallery's Collection. In 1823 he was nominated together with William Ashford and William Cuming to select members for the new Royal Hibernian Academy. He died in 1826, the same year in which eight of his oils and two watercolours were exhibited at the inaugural Royal Hibernian Exhibition.

Although Roberts' work in oils was not quite as fine as that of his brother, *A Landscape,* signed T.S.R., is an accomplished scene. Thomas Sautelle was, however, a master of the small-scale watercolour, several examples of which are in the Gallery's Collection. The view in this picture represents no specific location, as it is an idealised landscape. On stylistic grounds it represents a mature work; Roberts skilfully employs a thick, well-laden brush to the painting of the river and surrounding landscape, and this technique imparts great life and energy to the scene. Essentially a warm and windswept landscape, attractive features such as the playful and wayward goats and the contented image of the shepherd overseeing the animals, add a lively touch to this scene.

William Sadler II (c.1782-1839)

THE PIGEON HOUSE, DUBLIN c.1800

Oil on panel,
29 x 41cm
NGI NO. 632

THIS VIEW, one of two by William Sadler II in the Collection of the National Gallery of Ireland, depicts the Pigeon House, Dublin, and beside it a military fort which is located behind sandbag emplacements. A Union Jack flutters in the breeze, high above the building complex. During the eighteenth century Ringsend served as the port to Dublin, with the Pigeon House and the military fort prominently placed, until the north wall and other improvements made Dublin port safe. Towards the end of the century, the port was enlarged and linked to the Grand Canal. The basin, on the left of the wall, was under construction in 1790. In this scene, a number of vessels of different kinds are moored. The elaborate decoration on the bow of one of these ships has been carefully delineated and serves to lead the eye of the viewer towards the background of the picture where the buildings are situated. The artist has paid attention to the detail in his portrayal of the buildings. The Pigeon House can be seen to have classically inspired architectural features, including columns flanking the entrance, stringcourse marking the division between upper and lower level, and pedimented windows. The more austere military fort offers a striking contrast in design, as do the outhouses close by. The route leading to this area is depicted as a busy thoroughfare. Soldiers can be seen returning with a wagon to the fort. One man leans over the wall with a telescope to view the anchored ships and boats at closer range. All this evidence of life adds anecdotal interest to the scene.

Sadler was born in Dublin about 1782, the son of the portrait painter William Sadler. It is known that he depicted many views of Dublin during his career and also executed many copies of the old masters. The artist contributed to the various exhibitions in Dublin, including the Royal Hibernian Academy. His works, which are considerable in number, are generally of small size and painted on mahogany panels. They are remarkable for their sharp attention to detail and delicacy of finish. This small view is of the oddly named Pigeon House. The building became a lodging house in the mid eighteenth century and was run by a John Pidgeon, from whose name it is thought to have derived. Towards the end of the century, with increasing political tensions developing in Ireland and abroad, it became a military base, providing a landing place for troops.

John Comerford (c.1762-c.1823)

PORTRAIT OF ROBERT EMMET c.1802/3

Watercolour on
ivory,
6.9 x 5.7 cm
NGI NO. 7341

THE SUBJECT of this portrait miniature is Robert Emmet (1778-1803), a young Protestant who was born in Dublin and later became leader of the rebellion against British power in Ireland. His father was physician to the viceroy. He entered Trinity College Dublin, where his brother Thomas Addis Emmet had already excelled. Emmet's career at University was particularly notable. He was an outstanding orator, taking the nationalist side on political motions. He became involved with the Society of United Irishmen, but his political activities came to the attention of John Fitzgibbon, the lord chancellor, as a result of which he fled to the Continent on the eve of the 1798 Rising. He tried unsuccessfully in 1802 to interest Napoleon and Tallyrand in supporting another rebellion.

He returned to Ireland, making plans for a revolution, resolving to succeed where Wolfe Tone had failed. He reorganised the United Irishmen and planned to storm Dublin Castle. On the appointed day, 23 July 1803, Emmet set out for the Castle with a hundred followers. In Thomas Street they came across Lord Kilwarden, who was the chief justice and a fair-minded judge, and they killed him and his nephew. At first Emmet fled to the Dublin mountains but later returned to take his farewell of his fiancée, Sarah Curran, daughter of John Philpot Curran (who disapproved of the liaison). Emmet was betrayed to the authorities, arrested, tried and found guilty of treason. His extraordinary speech from the dock contained the inspirational words: *'I have but one request to make...Let no man write my epitaph... When my country takes her place among the nations of the earth, then, and not till then, let my epitaph be written'.* Emmet was only twenty-four when he died.

The Kilkenny-born artist John Comerford trained at the Dublin Society Drawing Schools in the 1780s, where he won a silver medal for figure drawing in 1791. He was greatly influenced by the English painter George Chinnery (1774-1852), who lived in Ireland from 1795 to 1802, and possibly also by Gilbert Stuart (1755-1828), the American portrait painter who worked in Ireland during the years 1787-93. Comerford was moderately successful as a portrait painter in oils when he decided, as a result of meeting Chinnery, to specialise in miniatures. Miniatures are small portable portraits with a private, commemorative and decorative function. Comerford used the popular eighteenth-century technique of luminous watercolour on ivory, which reflected beautifully on its polished surface. His heads are well drawn and finely modelled in grey hatching, which gives a soft effect, and he liked to use a reddish brown shade in painting the sitter's face. His work is important in the evolution of Irish portrait painting and he had considerable effect on his pupils. He was unusual among his contemporaries in being able to obtain all his commissions in Ireland, many of whom were from famous personages such as Daniel O'Connell and members of the Butler (Ormonde) family. This miniature is a copy of a sketch made by John Comerford during the trial of Robert Emmet in 1803 and was presented to the Irish nation by the Emmet family. It was created to commemorate a significant historical event.

Adam Buck (1759-1833)

PORTRAIT OF A LADY WITH AN ARTIST'S FOLIO 1803

Watercolour on
paper,
39 x 29 cm
NGI NO. 7738

THIS PORTRAIT SHOWS an elegant young woman, hair piled high, wearing a muslin gown, standing on a terrace. The late-eighteenth-century spirit of liberty encouraged fashion to reflect the style of the first Roman republic; the sitter wears a high-waisted dress with simple lines, showing this influence of neo-classicism. Developments in the textile industry resulted in muslin being much more readily available. These new fashionable 'loose' styles (made of white muslin imported from the new colonies in India) became the uniform of femininity. The young woman is about to open a blue portfolio for inspection. The way in which her head is held proudly aloft and the determined expression on her face alerts us to the fact that she is a conscientious student and is seeking a proper and serious appreciation of her work. The painting, which dates from 1803, is from an era when young women were encouraged to take up drawing, but strictly as a pastime, and their artistic endeavours tended to be regarded solely as a graceful feminine accomplishment. Females who wished to pursue professional art training faced many obstacles with regard to studying and gaining critical approval. It was not until the mid nineteenth century that they were admitted to art schools. It would be more than a century before the work of women artists would be considered with the same respect as that of men.

The delicacy of execution which distinguishes this watercolour is in keeping with the fact that the artist, Adam Buck, was an accomplished miniature painter, as well as being a master of this type of small full-length portrait. Some of his portraits were painted in watercolour, others in wax crayon. Born in Cork, the eldest son of a silversmith, he worked as a miniaturist and painter of small full-length portraits in Cork, where he evolved his own decorative neo-classical style. In 1795 he moved permanently to London. He exhibited regularly at the Royal Academy and other important public art venues in the city. His sitters were mostly politicians, clergy, theatre people and military officers. The design of the wrought-iron balustrade behind the figure, and of the chair, is influenced by classical Greek motifs. Buck was deeply interested in antique Greek and Roman vase painting, which influenced his choice of portraying the figure in profile. He published a prospectus for a book on Greek vase painting in 1811.

James Barry (1741-1806)

SELF-PORTRAIT AS TIMANTHES, 1780-1803

Oil on canvas,
76 x 63 cm
NGI NO. 971

J AMES BARRY came from Cork, and after initial training went on to attend the Dublin Society Schools. While he was in Dublin he came to the attention of Edmund Burke, who recognised Barry's talent and financed his journeys to Rome and Paris, after which Barry settled in London in 1771. He quickly established himself as the leading painter of historical subjects on a monumental scale. Despite being a highly successful history painter, Barry had a difficult and troubled life, and died impoverished in London. In his arresting self-portrait, he likens himself to the Greek artist Timanthes. Barry chose Timanthes because, having won in competition with Ajax, Timanthes had incurred the envy of his contemporaries, hence the classical reference to Hercules crushing the snake of envy. It was in 1780 that Barry began painting the head of this self-portrait. It was intended as a model for his representation as Timanthes in the huge mural, the *Crowning of the Victors*, for the Society of Arts, London. In his hand, Barry holds his recreation of one of Timanthes' lost paintings: *The Cyclops and the Satyrs*, showing Satyrs cautiously approaching a sleeping Cyclops. In this way, Barry associated himself with a renowned work by an ancient master.

Work began in 1774 on the decorative scheme of which the *Crowning of the Victors* was a part, and Barry dedicated himself to this project for the next six years without payment. He was one of the leading history painters in Britain, and in 1779 was appointed Professor of Painting at the Royal Academy. Through a combination of his radical political beliefs and eccentric behaviour, he was expelled from the Academy in 1799. By the time he had completed the present portrait in 1803, Barry's fortunes had radically declined. As a way of honouring the artist, The Society of Arts suggested having his self-portrait engraved as the frontispiece of their *Transactions*. Barry offered them this self-portrait, which depicts a dramatic image of himself as the heroic artist. This serious and solemn portrait reflects his artistic profession, evidenced by the drawing implement in his hand, the classical tradition that informed his work, represented below by the base of the statue of Hercules trampling on the serpent of Envy, and the inclusion of the Cyclops painting, which enabled him to associate himself with a renowned ancient master. Barry felt he did not receive the recognition he deserved for his art. The anguished expression refers to his feeling that he was different to others, while the pose and manner create the image of a solitary romantic artist.

Samuel Frederick Brocas (c.1792-1847)

TRINITY COLLEGE AND COLLEGE GREEN, DUBLIN 1818

Ink and watercolour
on paper,
24.4 x 40.2 cm
NGI NO. 2558

THIS VIEW of Trinity College and College Green by Samuel Brocas illustrates the artist's interest in people and architecture. The façade of the West Front of Trinity College Dublin is one of a number of projects designed in the eighteenth century with a view to creating a beautiful city centre. The college was founded by Queen Elizabeth I on the site of an Augustinian Priory, All Hallows, in 1592, but it only received its splendid façade in the second half of the 1750s. The building was designed by Theodore Jacobson (d.1772), a gentleman architect, and the stone carving was done by James Robinson. Wicklow granite was used to face the building, in accordance with the Palladian practice of employing local materials, and the more pliable Portland stone for the intricate decorative carving. The style is Palladian, based upon the work and theory of Andrea Palladio (1518-80), who imitated ancient Roman architecture. His theory, formulated in his *Four Books on Architecture* (1570), was extremely popular in England at the end of the seventeenth century and during the first half of the eighteenth century. The architectural features that make up the façade, in particular the impressive portico front and balustraded end pavilions, indicate that the architect had fully absorbed the ideas of Palladio.

Samuel Frederick Brocas was born into an artistic family around 1792, with no less than six artists bearing the Brocas name working successfully in Dublin in the first half of the nineteenth century. He was a landscape painter in oils and watercolour, who exhibited at the Royal Hibernian Academy between 1828 and 1847. A number of topographical views point to his having travelled in England, Wales and Scotland. Twelve of his celebrated views of Dublin, executed in watercolour and pencil, were engraved by his brother Henry Brocas the Younger (1798-1873), and issued between 1818 and 1829. They were part of a proposed series of views of Ireland which were never realised. Here Brocas records the façade of the College with swift pen-strokes, over which is applied light washes of colour. He also observes how light falls on the building, creating light and shadows, rendering it an even more effective model. Smoke can be seen coming from the chimneys, giving a lived-in appearance to the College. Brocas was very interested in the social interaction around buildings, hence life on the busy streets outside is graphically captured in this painting. A carriage rolls by, with others seen in the distance. Two gentlemen riders progress at stately pace on their mounts, while close by a well-dressed couple in the height of fashion stroll contentedly. The small detail of a man carrying a load is included to remind us that this is a city of work as well as of study and leisure.

Martin Archer Shee (1769-1850)

THOMAS MOORE, POET (1779-1852) 1820s

Oil on canvas,
91 x 70 cm
NGI NO. 775

Thomas moore, the poet, was born in Dublin and graduated with a Bachelor of Arts degree from Trinity College in 1798. While at Trinity he formed a close friendship with the United Irishman Robert Emmet. The poet went to London in 1799 to study law. An accomplished harpsichordist, he was a favourite figure on the social scene. It did not take long for him to establish a literary reputation, beginning with the publication of his *Odes of Anacreon* in 1800. He is best remembered today for his *Irish Melodies*, published in a series of ten volumes (1807-34). He often sang these songs while accompanying himself with piano or harp. Full of Irish sentiment, they proved to be highly popular with English and Irish audiences.

This portrait depicts Moore in his role as man of letters. With no private income, he was dependent on writing for his living. His poem *Lalla Rookh* (1817), on which Daniel Maclise based a painting, won him the largest sum ever paid for a poem at the time. In Shee's portrait, he is seated by a table on which are placed some books and sheaves of paper. The paper is blank, and the pose and expression of the sitter suggest that Moore is in the process of working through an idea in his head before putting pen to paper. The head is raised, the mouth is slightly parted and the eyes are focused somewhere in the middle distance. Deep in thought, Moore leans back slightly in the chair, resting his elbow on the table as he does so. He dangles an eye-glass in his hand, while in his mind he ponders ideas, words and rhythm. That we are in the presence of a successful man is indicated both by the cut of his garments and by the inclusion of rich, heavy drapery close to the chair. The palette chosen by the artist is a mixture of warm browns and golden yellows. Touches of red and violet are also used. He unifies the composition very effectively through colour. Note how the violet of the tablecloth is repeated in the blush of the sitter's cheek and the deep brown of the frock-coat is echoed in lighter tones on the wall behind.

Born in Dublin, Martin Archer Shee attended the Dublin Society Schools. Even before his twentieth birthday he was a successfully employed portrait painter. He arrived in London in 1788 and in no time his patrons covered a very wide range of society. He was much sought after in literary circles, as evidenced by this portrait. In 1800 he was elected a full member of the Royal Academy. Thirty years later he was elected President of the Academy and was subsequently knighted.

John George Mulvany (c.1766-1838)

KILMALLOCK, CO. LIMERICK c.1820

Oil on canvas,
68 x 80 cm
NGI NO. 991

THIS VIEW of Kilmallock by John George Mulvany shows the medieval magnificance of the walled town with its gates. A busy market town in the south of Co. Limerick, Kilmallock owes its origins to the Normans. It was a Geraldine town, one of the most splendid and wealthy in Ireland, and was the capital of Munster. It was significant enough to return two members of parliament until the Act of Union of 1800. By the time a population survey of the town was published in 1837, listing all 1,213 inhabitants, Kilmallock had become run-down. Mulvany's view of the main street and sixteenth-century King's Castle represents an important record of the once great, prosperous, chief town of the earls of Desmond. The picture illustrates Blossom's Gate, one of only two of the original four medieval gates which were still standing. The Tudor houses with mullioned windows, shown in ruined condition on either side of the street, have since all been demolished. An interesting aspect of Mulvany's picture is the amount of anecdotal detail, such as the lodging house where the sheets are being aired at the window, the tavern with its sign, and the linen and drapery shop. The statistical surveys carried out by the Dublin Society indicated that in the early nineteenth century, people were reasonably well dressed, a fact confirmed by this picture, where the townspeople are shown in their everyday clothes actively engaged in their daily business.

John George Mulvany was trained at the Dublin Society Schools, winning medals in 1782 and 1786. He is recorded as having been a very successful artist and is chiefly remembered as a landscapist. He taught for most of his life and exhibited some genre scenes in watercolour. One of the characteristics of his work is a smooth painting surface and attention to detail. His inclusion of anecdotal detail, such as people in rural settings with animals, as illustrated in this view of Kilmallock, adds great life and interest to the scene. When the Royal Hibernian Academy was established in 1823, Mulvany was invited to become a founder member. The picture is discreetly signed by the artist on the signboard above the tavern.

Thomas Kirk (1781-1845)

PORTRAIT OF RICHARD BRINSLEY SHERIDAN (1751-1816), DRAMATIST AND POLITICIAN 1824

Marble,
72 cm ht.
NGI NO. 8000

RICHARD BRINSLEY SHERIDAN was born in Dublin in 1751. His father, Thomas Sheridan, was manager of the Theatre Royal in Smock Alley; his mother, Frances Sheridan, was a novelist and playwright. The family moved to England in 1759, and Richard Brinsley never returned to Ireland. He eloped to France in 1772 with Elizabeth Linley, a young singer, in a bid to save her from an arranged marriage. Two duels were fought over this woman by Sheridan and the man she was supposed to marry. One year later she married Sheridan. The warm reception of plays such as *The Rivals* (1775) and *The School for Scandal* (1777) resulted in his early success as a playwright. As manager of the Theatre Royal in Drury Lane, he played an influential role in the theatrical life of London. However, he also had a deep interest in public affairs. In 1780 he became MP for Stafford, holding minor offices in Whig governments. He was sympathetic to the American and French revolutions and opposed the Union of Great Britain and Ireland. His high lifestyle and the burning down of his theatre in 1809 almost landed him in the debtors' prison. A public subscription rescued him from this fate. He died in 1816 and was buried in the Poets' Corner at Westminster Abbey.

Thomas Kirk sculpted this bust, comprising a head and shoulders of Sheridan, eight years after his death. To make the likeness a convincing one, he relied on images produced during Sheridan's lifetime, including paintings, drawings and prints. Sheridan is depicted in serious, thoughtful mood. He is dressed in classical garb rather than contemporary costume, which was the standard sculptural treatment for a bust in the neo-classical style. This device was to indicate that the person portrayed was someone worthy of fame, not just in his own age, but for all ages. The carving of the features is delicately handled and a pleasing contrast is achieved between the smooth flesh, the tight, crisply rendered curls and flowing sweep of drapery. Kirk, born in Cork, was commissioned in 1808 to execute the statue of Nelson for the Pillar which dominated O'Connell Street, Dublin. He also carried out numerous other public monuments and enjoyed success as a portrait sculptor. His busts were considered to be true likenesses of his sitters. A founder member of the Royal Hibernian Academy, he regularly exhibited there up until his death in 1845.

Francis Danby (1793-1861)

THE OPENING OF THE SIXTH SEAL 1828

Oil on canvas,
185 x 255 cm
NGI NO. 162

And I beheld, when he had opened the sixth seal, and, lo! there was a great earthquake; and the sun became black as sackcloth of hair, and the moon became as blood: And the stars of heaven fell unto the earth, even as a fig-tree casteth her untimely figs, when she is shaken of a mighty wind. And the heaven departed as a scroll when it is rolled together; and every mountain and island were moved out of their places. And the kings of the earth, and the great men, and the rich men, and the chief captains, and the mighty men and every bondman and every free man hid themselves in the dens and in the rocks of the mountains; and said to the mountains and rocks, Fall on us, and hide us from the face of Him that sitteth on the throne, and from the wrath of the Lamb; For the great day of His wrath is come; and who shall be able to stand. (Revelations 6: 12-17)

*T*he *Opening of the Sixth Seal* portrays the earth opening up and bursting into disarray. The sky is lit up unnaturally in an otherwise darkened world. A volcano has erupted with such violence that rocks are hurled into the air, lava spills forth, and lightning strikes a craggy hillside with huge force. Cities collapse and their inhabitants call upon the mountains to fall on them and hide them from the wrath of God. This catastrophic event is based on lines from the Book of Revelations which vividly describe the day of wrath. In keeping with the subject matter, the artist chose a very large canvas. By this means he could render the scene as dramatically as possible and impress upon the viewer the terrors of nature unleashed. In dramatic works such as these, Danby displays his awareness of a broad romantic movement sweeping across Europe in the nineteenth century. The artist employs a palette of darkest browns, fiery reds and startling contrast of creamy whites and grey, that vividly conjure up the scene. The sheer scale of the landscape, when measured against the puniness of the figures, forcefully conveys the idea that human beings are not in control of the world they inhabit. Only one person in the picture, a slave, is still standing. His chains are broken and he is finally free. The picture is not solely a visual interpretation of the opening of the sixth seal, but is also a statement against slavery, the abolishment of which was a burning issue in the 1820s.

Francis Danby was a master of spectacular scenes. Indeed this painting proved to be so popular when exhibited in the Royal Academy (London) Exhibition of 1828 that it was moved to a separate gallery because of the huge crowds it attracted. The artist was born in Co. Wexford, studied at the Dublin Society Drawing Schools and began his career painting landscapes. In 1813 he went to London, along with two other landscape painters, James Arthur O'Connor and George Petrie. Of the three, Danby settled in Bristol, the other two artists returning to Ireland. Despite declaring himself 'an English artist', his work shows the influence of James Arthur O'Connor and earlier eighteenth-century Irish landscape painters.

James Arthur O'Connor (1792-1841)

A THUNDERSTORM: THE FRIGHTENED WAGONER 1832

Oil on canvas,
65 x 76 cm
NGI NO. 4041

A Thunderstorm: The Frightened Wagoner is a superb example of a romantic landscape painting and is regarded as one of the artist's finest works. James Arthur O'Connor was born in Dublin. It seems that he was self-taught as an artist. He became friendly with two fellow painters, George Petrie and Francis Danby, and they went to London together in 1813. There was little patronage in Ireland at this time and all three hoped to establish successful careers in England. After some months O'Connor was obliged to come home to support his orphaned sisters. He remained in the country for about ten years, working as a landscape artist painting a number of estates in the west of Ireland. In 1822 he returned to London. He exhibited at major exhibition venues, showing landscapes, including Irish scenes. Major influences on his landscape style included seventeenth-century Dutch landscapists, the French painter Claude Lorrain, and the eighteenth-century English artist Thomas Gainsborough. O'Connor's later subject matter was dominated by magnificent landscapes, of which this picture is a perfect example.

The mood of the scene is set immediately by the giant twisting tree in the left foreground. It struggles to remain rooted to the ground against the ferocity of the wind, which whips at the branches and leaves. The sky is rent apart by a bolt of lightning. Close by is a cascading waterfall. The theatrical quality of the scene is further enhanced by the wagon-driver standing helplessly beside his wagon. The puny scale of the figure set against the impressive height of the craggy mountain-top and the gigantic tree indicates clearly the vulnerability of humans in the face of the unleashing of the forces of nature. Animals are known to have an unerring sense of danger, and the reaction of the horses to having to cross the bridge adds to the mood of danger in the picture. The artist adds another dimension to the picture of the frightened wagoner by means of agitated brushwork, a heightened sense of movement and the dramatic treatment of light.

It is thought that O'Connor's treatment of the subject may have been directly inspired by William Wordsworth's poem 'The Wagoner', which was published in 1819. One quotation from the poem goes as follows:

> *The rain rushed down — the road was battered,*
> *As with the force of billows shattered;*
> *The horses are dismayed, nor know*
> *Whether they should stand or go.*

Patrick MacDowell (1799-1870)

A GIRL READING 1838

Marble,
141 cm ht.
NGI NO. 8250

THIS CHARMING FIGURE sculpture carved by Patrick MacDowell in 1838 portrays the full-length figure of a young girl intent on her book; the loose robe she wears has fallen from her shoulders, in folds that reveal the graceful body beneath. Her naturally curling locks, held in place with braided ribbon in the classical style, cascade down the back of her swanlike neck. Her prettiness is evident in the perfection of the profile, her gently lowered eyes, the soft curve of the mouth. The tapering fingers which hold the book in shape also enhance her natural elegance. Rather than represent an individual, the sculptor has created a type, in which the grace and refinement of youth are duly celebrated in marble. It is also a representation of the enthusiasm of middle- and upper-class women for novels. The carving is sensitively executed; the diaphanous folds of drapery are lightly incised and provide an interesting contrast to the more deeply gouged coiling hair.

Patrick MacDowell was born in Belfast in 1799 and while still an infant went to live in England. In 1813 he was apprenticed to a coach-builder in London, who became bankrupt. At that time MacDowell happened to be lodging in the home of a sculptor, P.F. Chenu, and with his encouragement he began to draw and model. In 1830 he entered the Royal Academy's School and succeeded in travelling to Rome ten years later. He was by then an established sculptor, employed not only on portrait busts but also executing imaginative statues and statuettes. Among his most important works is his statue to the painter Joseph Mallord William Turner (1775-1851) in St Paul's Cathedral, London. MacDowell was elected an associate of the Royal Academy in 1841, and made a full member in 1846. A popular sculptor in his own lifetime, he had a reputation for producing finely designed figures, full of touching sentiment, in the conventional neo-classical idiom.

George Petrie (1790-1866)

THE LAST CIRCUIT OF PILGRIMS AT CLONMACNOISE, CO. OFFALY c.1838

Pencil and water-
colour on paper,
67.2 x 98 cm
NGI NO. 2230

GEORGE PETRIE was a versatile character, being not alone a painter, antiquary, musician and writer, but also a collector of folklore and pioneer in systematic and scientific approaches to Irish history and archaeology. The son of a miniature painter and portraitist, Petrie trained at the Dublin Society Schools and early in his career undertook sketching trips around Ireland, his main interest being the study of archaeological remains. During the 1820s he produced numerous illustrations for Cromwell's *Excursions Around Ireland* and other travel books. Petrie mixed in a wide circle of learned and artistic people, which included his biographer, William Stokes. In 1828 he became a member of the Royal Irish Academy, for which he worked assiduously to acquire manuscripts and antiquities, while also publishing on Irish traditional music and archaeology. During 1833-41 he headed the topographical department of the Ordnance Survey. Petrie became a member of the RHA in 1828, the first watercolourist so honoured, and he reigned briefly as President.

Although Petrie first visited Clonmacnoise in 1818, executing over three hundred drawings of the site, his earliest illustration, *The Last Round of the Pilgrims at Clonmacnoise*, was made in 1828 for a Mrs Haldiman. When he came to compose the work illustrated here, he rearranged the grouping of the key features, such as the round tower, Cross of the Scriptures and the banks of the river Shannon, to achieve a more picturesque effect! In a letter to the Royal Irish Art Union about 1838, he explained that he wished to produce a picture, historical in object and poetical in sentiment, that would link ancient historic monuments destined for destruction with the fate of the Irish people. Although the watercolour has faded, it is still one of Petrie's finest pieces. This monastic settlement of Clonmacnoise was a sixth-century site established by St Ciarán. It was attacked frequently during the Middle Ages, and what now remains is the ruins of the cathedral, two high crosses, a round tower and six churches. The title, *The Last Circuit of Pilgrims at Clonmacnoise*, refers to a nineteenth-century practice of visiting holy sites on 'pattern-day', in this case the feast-day of St Ciarán (d. AD 545) in June, when pilgrims would gather at Clonmacnoise to pray to the saint. The manner in which Petrie has grouped the figures around the ruined monuments, set against the fading sunset, is evocative. This picture is an important record of a significant site. While demonstrating Petrie's absorption with Ireland's historic past and illustrating his sadness at the passing of Celtic Ireland, it is also a testment to the continuity and survival of religious faith.

William Mulready (1786-1863)

STUDY FOR 'THE SONNET' 1839

Pencil and red chalk
with white highlights
on paper,
36 x 29.9 cm
NGI NO. 2950

The season's paintings do not please, Gentlemen,
Like Etty, Mulready or Maclise;
Throbbing romance has waned and wanned.
(Thomas Hardy, *An Ancient to Ancient,* 1922)

THIS DRAWING, dating to 1839, is a finished cartoon for the composition *The Sonnet,* which William Mulready painted in the same year for his most important patron, the well-known English collector John Sheepshanks. The subject of the study is a young couple who are romantically involved. They share a moment as the girl reads a sonnet presented by the shy young man. The drawing is successful in conveying the tension of the situation, as the young man nervously anticipates the reaction to his gift, while his companion attempts to stifle a smile at the sentiments expressed in the poem. The artist believed in the importance of carefully worked-up preparatory studies prior to executing his highly finished panel paintings. Hallmarks of Mulready's style are evident here in his attention to the finely drawn figures and the sensitively outlined pastoral setting. The design for *The Sonnet* differs only marginally from the finished panel, now in the Victoria and Albert Museum, London. The painting was also the subject of an engraving issued in 1840 by The Royal Irish Art Union.

William Mulready was born in Ennis, Co. Clare, and by the age of five the family moved, first to Dublin and then in 1792 to London. From an early age Mulready showed a precocious talent for drawing. He trained first with the sculptor Thomas Banks before enrolling in 1800 at the Royal Academy Schools. There he came under the influence of John Varley, who encouraged him to try landscapes. By the age of eighteen he began exhibiting at the Royal Academy, where he continued to exhibit almost every year until his death in 1863. On the advice of David Wilkie, Mulready turned from landscape to subject painting, with scenes of everyday life based on the Dutch seventeenth-century masters. An extremely successful genre painter, he illustrated small, domestic narrative scenes, and had a particular gift for themes which illustrated children. These richly coloured compositions were beautifully crafted, with an emphasis on drawing and attention to detail, factors that were to influence the young Pre-Raphaelites. He was elected an associate of the Royal Academy in 1815, and was made a full RA the following year. In 1839 Mulready was commissioned by Henry Cole, then assistant to Rowland Hill, the inventor of the penny post office, to design the first pre-paid postage envelope, which was called the Mulready postal envelope and issued in 1840. Mulready became one of the most successful Victorian genre painters and his achievements brought him fame and recognition, notably in 1855 when he was awarded the *Légion d'honneur,* having exhibited at the Exposition Universelle in Paris.

Trevor Thomas Fowler (fl.1829-44)

CHILDREN DANCING AT A CROSSROADS c.1840

Oil on canvas,
71 x 92 cm
NGI NO. 4122

NINETEENTH-CENTURY PAINTING is noted for the predominance of anecdotal, sentimental images. The majority of Fowler's known works are genre pictures, such as *Children Dancing at a Crossroads*, which depicts an everyday scene in the country. It is cheerful and lively, suggesting the sound of the dancing, the music of the flute and reflecting the energy of the dancers' movements. The composition is simple, with figures in the foreground and a sketchily outlined landscape in the background, which has no distinguishing features to identify the location. The theme of the picture, children dancing, represents a common pastime at crossroads throughout Ireland at that time. This type of informal gathering provided an opportunity for young people to meet and socialise. The artist shows that his real interest lies in the people; as is evident throughout in details such as the seated old woman smoking a clay pipe, the boy drinking, and the profile of the child listening to the musician. The picture incorporates a variety of figures wearing traditional, homespun costumes, including colourful shawls, hats and waistjackets made from a mixture of frieze, flannel, coarse linen and wool. Despite their evident poverty, the young people are presented as being well fed, happy and healthy, and while this is a somewhat idealised view of their situation, it is in keeping with nineteenth-century views on art, which discouraged artists from portraying the harsher realities of life.

Very little is known about the career of Trevor Fowler. He began exhibiting at the Royal Hibernian Academy in 1830 and continued showing work most years up to 1844; his address was listed in Dublin, except for 1843 when he submitted three works from Paris. In 1843 he showed *La Jeune Artiste* at the Royal Irish Art Union Exhibition in Dublin, for which he won a prize. His output included portraits, subject pictures and views of the river Barrow, Co. Kilkenny and Co. Carlow. Fowler is recorded as being an associate of the RHA, and his subject pictures, such as the one illustrated here, bear some affinity to genre paintings by William Mulready (1786-1863).

Joseph P. Haverty (1794-1864)

THE BLIND PIPER 1840s

Oil on canvas,
76 x 59 cm
NGI NO. 166

*T*he Blind Piper, also known as *The Limerick Piper*, is the most famous work by Thomas Patrick Haverty, lithographs of which can still be found around Ireland. Haverty came from Galway, and presumably received his training there, before moving to Dublin. He travelled in search of work, visiting London on several occasions. On his return to Dublin he was made an associate member in 1823 of the newly established Royal Hibernian Academy, becoming a full member in 1829. He was a successful portrait painter and depicted the prominent political figure, Daniel O'Connell, on numerous occasions. Haverty also painted narrative subject pictures, several of which have nationalist and religious overtones. The National Gallery's *Father Mathew receiving a Repentant Pledge-Breaker* by the artist has a strong moral theme.

One of the reasons why *The Blind Piper* is also known as *The Limerick Piper* is because Haverty, although based in Dublin, spent several years in that city. *The Limerick Piper* was engraved in 1847 and distributed in 1848 by the Royal Irish Art Union. The subject of the painting is Patrick O'Brien, who was born in Co. Clare about 1773, the son of a farmer. Having lost his sight at the age of twenty-six, he followed in the tradition of blind musicians by learning to play the uileann pipes in order to support himself. He was also known to be very proud of his linguistic abilities in Irish, English and Latin. O'Brien moved to Limerick city, where his regular spot was at the corner of Hartstonge Street and the Crescent. In all probability this is where Haverty first saw him and persuaded him to sit for a portrait.

Haverty depicts the piper realistically as a proud old man. While his clothing is respectable, he is certainly not dressed as a gentleman. He is seen wearing a heavy, navy-blue, woollen knee-length coat with brown trousers, a white shirt with soft black cravat, blue stockings and black brogues. His overcoat is torn and mended, his trousers look worn and his socks are untidy. O'Brien cuts a strong and dignified figure and is shown totally absorbed in some melancholic air. Tradition tells us that the girl in the picture was the piper's daughter, and she is shown wearing a red petticoat and white top, probably of a woollen-linen mixture. She sits with a thoughtful air beside her father, toes curled up at the fire. If their circumstances had been more comfortable, she might have been portrayed with a cloak and wearing shoes. It is a sensitive if sentimental portrayal of a young child. Haverty sets the scene within a windswept autumnal landscape to convey a romantic analogy of nature, quite unlike the urban reality of the piper's normal situation.

Frederic William Burton (1816-1900)

THE ARAN FISHERMAN'S DROWNED CHILD 1841

Watercolour on
paper,
88.4 x 78.5 cm
NGI NO. 6048

The Aran Fisherman's Drowned Child was painted by Frederic Burton in 1841, exhibited in Dublin and London in 1842, and became a popular print when it was published by the Royal Irish Art Union in 1843. It is one of a number of early west of Ireland subject pictures by Burton, and is significant in serving as a visual record of the pre-Famine period. The picture, while dramatically documenting a tragic event, is executed in the manner of mid-nineteenth-century romantic painting. The scene is of the mother, family, friends and professional keeners (mourners) gathered around the figure of the dead child. The most striking figure in the picture is the father, who stands immobile, fraught with grief, staring outward. Other people wearing cloaks and sailing costumes enter the cabin to be told of the sad event. Burton executed up to fifty preparatory studies for this work, and a preliminary watercolour sketch portrays the father in a more natural pose than in the finished version. Burton's antiquarian background led him to make accurate records of western lifestyle, as is demonstrated here in the precise detailing of costumes, furniture and folklore, and references to traditions and customs of the west of Ireland. While he knew the west intimately, there is no record of him having visited the Aran Islands before 1857, when he was part of the British Association expedition. It is most likely that the artist used somewhere familiar to him, such as the old Claddagh village beside Galway, for the location of the scene. *The Aran Fisherman's Drowned Child* is the major work of Burton's early career and a superb example of his skill as a watercolourist.

Frederic William Burton was born in Corofin, Co. Clare, the son of an amateur landscape painter. The family moved to Dublin in 1826, where Burton attended the Dublin Society Schools, studying under Robert West and Henry Brocas Senior. He first exhibited at the RHA in 1832 and by 1839 had become a full academician. Burton started out as a miniature painter under the influence of John Comerford and Samuel Lover. He achieved early success through his refined technique, his style following that of contemporary Irish miniaturists, who employed watercolour on ivory and adopted the popular form of head and shoulders within an oval shape. Miniature painting provided useful training for Burton, who was later able to apply some of these techniques to full-scale portraiture and genre pictures. Burton had an enquiring mind, he was interested in art history, and through his friendship with George Petrie, the noted topographical painter, he mixed with leading antiquaries, like Thomas Davis, Eugene O'Curry, Samuel Ferguson and William Stokes. He became a member of the Royal Society of Antiquaries and was a founder member of the Archaeological Society of Ireland.

John Hogan (1800-58)

HIBERNIA WITH A BUST OF LORD CLONCURRY 1844

Marble,
148 cm ht.
(on loan to the
National Gallery
of Ireland)
NGI NO. 14,688

THIS MARBLE GROUP was sculpted by John Hogan in 1844 while he was living in Rome (between the years 1823 and 1848). It depicts Hibernia (Ireland), with a coronet and laurel leaves. She is seated on a chair of antique design. By her side is a harp and at her feet an Irish wolfhound, some books, a scroll, and an inverted crown decorated with a shamrock. The figure of Hibernia was a frequently employed motif, used to symbolise Ireland in wrought-iron work and stucco in eighteenth- and nineteenth-century buildings and metalwork. She has her arm around the bust of Valentine Lawless, Lord Cloncurry. The bust forms the top of a Herm, a motif drawn from classical antiquity. The features of the portrait have been modelled sensitively in a more idealised than realistic manner. At the time the work was being carried out, Cloncurry was in his late sixties, yet the sculptor chose not to emphasise the wrinkles of advancing age. He also treats the bust in the manner of the antique, leaving the eyes unincised and the hair brushed forward. The group was commissioned by Cloncurry, who saw himself as an Irish patriot, and above the usual petty political rivalries. He had joined the United Irishmen and was several times imprisoned. He supported Catholic Emancipation and the abolition of tithes and was active in attempts to provide relief during the Famine of 1845-50. He also saw himself as a patron of the arts and travelled extensively on the Continent. Cloncurry proved to be a supportive patron during the period of the commission. For instance, anxious that Hibernia's harp be authentically designed, he sent the sculptor an old coin with an Irish harp on it.

The sculptor, John Hogan, was born in Tallow, Co. Waterford, in 1800, but the family moved to Cork one year after his birth. In 1823, thanks to cash support from a number of enthusiasts and patrons of his work, he was enabled to go to Italy, where he was to make his career. In 1829 he made his first return visit to Ireland and received several commissions. On the second return visit in 1832 he was presented with a gold medal at a special ceremony of the Cork Society for the Promotion of Fine Arts. He returned to Ireland on several more visits during his career and received a variety of commissions for busts, memorials and statues.

William Davis (1812-73)

A VIEW OF THE RYE WATER NEAR LEIXLIP c.1850

Oil on canvas,
51 x 76 cm
NGI NO. 4129

THE LANDSCAPE illustrated here was painted by Davis about 1850. The scene depicts the Rye, a small tributary river that joins the river Liffey just before Leixlip, about sixteen kilometres west of Dublin city. Known as the Rye Water, it is a small river which passes through some of the most attractive rural countryside in Co. Kildare. It rises near Kilcock and continues with Pebble Hill to one side and Carton Demesne on the other, flowing largely parallel to the Royal Canal to join the Liffey at Leixlip. The precise spot of the view illustrated here has not been identified. While Davis lived most of his life and made his career in Liverpool, he appears to have made a number of visits to his home near Leixlip. He exhibited at the Royal Hibernian Academy on three occasions between 1833 and 1856; one of these works listed, *Sketch near Leixlip*, was exhibited in 1856. *A View of the Rye Water near Leixlip* is an accomplished work, which clearly displays Davis' fine control of impasto paint and extremely precise brushwork. He shows great skill in his handling of light and shade and stunning assurance in the treatment of light reflecting on the water.

William Davis was not uncommon among Irish artists, including Richard Moynan and Nathaniel Hone the Younger, in starting out in one career and changing mid-course to train as a painter. In Davis' case he abandoned the study of law to attend the Dublin Society Schools. He established himself painting portraits and still life, but felt he was not making sufficient headway in Dublin, and at the age of twenty-three he left for Liverpool. In Liverpool he became an associate of the Academy in 1851, a full member in 1854, and in due course was appointed Professor of Drawing at the Academy. He is frequently grouped with Pre-Raphaelite painters, such as Ford Madox Brown and Holman Hunt, largely because some of his work is similar in style; he also painted landscapes and figure subjects displaying much in common with Robert Tonge. He exhibited his work frequently and with success at the Royal Academy in London.

William Osborne (1823-1901)

MARE AND FOAL 1850s

Oil on canvas,
50.5 x 69 cm
NGI NO. 4325

An ANIMAL-LOVER, William Osborne devoted himself to painting animals, mainly horses and dogs. In 1845 he entered the Royal Hibernian Academy as a student and first exhibited there in 1851 when he submitted two genre portraits of a boy and a girl and a painting of a dog. Although initially he tried to make a name in portraiture, he soon changed direction to portraying animals, chiefly dogs and horses. His pictures of dogs are full of life and based on a close study of the habits and characteristics of the animals. His pictures of horses include several hunting scenes, as well as some very fine individual portraits of the animals. The National Gallery of Ireland possesses a superb large, detailed composition, *The Ward Hunt*, which he painted in 1873. His son, Walter Osborne, became renowned as a portrait, landscape and genre painter.

This painting depicting a mare and foal is set outdoors. The horses are pictured outside a stable, its large entrance covered with a creeper. On the left, a half stable door is ajar. The day is fine, the mood tranquil. The horses fill the foreground of the picture. The sleek outlines of the creatures and their magnificent rich brown colouring are carefully realised in contrast to the more sketchily observed background. Osborne's sensitivity in portraying animals is especially evident in the painting of the horses' eyes. They are sharp, bright and intelligent and confer almost human personalities on the creatures. The foal, who nestles close to the mare, indicates a strong physical bond between both animals. Although not the only artist to concentrate on animals as subject matter in his art, William Osborne is regarded as one of the finest exponents of horse painting in Ireland in the nineteenth century, particularly in his individual portraits of these animals.

Henry McManus (c.1810-78)

READING '*THE NATION*' 1850s

Oil on canvas,
30.5 x 35.5 cm
NGI NO. 1917

Henry McManus came from Monaghan, and was a friend of Charles Gavan Duffy, a fellow townsman. His early known works are competent watercolours, with an emphasis on architecture and foreground figures. Later he worked as a portraitist, illustrator and watercolour landscapist. McManus was living in Dublin in 1836, by which time he had begun exhibiting at the Royal Hibernian Academy. The following year he moved to London, where he remained until 1844. In the 1840s he carried out a series of unsentimental genre illustrations for Hall's *Ireland*. In 1845 he was appointed Headmaster of the Glasgow School of Design, where he remained until 1849, when he returned to Ireland. He was appointed to the post of Headmaster at the School of Design in Dublin (1849-63), and during his term of office he instigated evening classes and day courses for women. He was a member from 1836 of the Belfast Association of Artists. McManus was elected Royal Hibernian Academician in 1858, he became Keeper in 1865, and for the remaining five years of his life was Professor of Painting. His obituary in *The Irish Times* stressed his teaching skills and his post as Headmaster of the Design School.

Reading 'The Nation' is McManus' best-known picture. It depicts an old man reading the current issue of *The Nation*, surrounded by a group of interested people who are listening and arguing. The newspaper was widely read and discussed around the country by groups of people, whether in the smithy, the pub, or after Mass on Sundays. The distinctive hooded cloaks of the women suggest the scene may be outside a church in the south of Ireland. Three members of Daniel O'Connell's Repeal Association, Thomas Davis, Charles Gavan Duffy and John Blake Dillon, founded *The Nation* in 1842 with the aim of: 'Creating and fostering public opinion in Ireland and making it racy of the soil'. The three also established the Young Ireland movement, which was dedicated to raising the consciousness of the Irish people in seeking political freedom. A significant feature of *The Nation* was the regular articles devoted to the arts and reviews of annual RHA exhibitions. McManus' association with Gavan Duffy resulted in the artist abandoning his unionist sympathies and embracing nationalism. He executed a number of portraits of well-known political figures, including several of Daniel O'Connell. This picture is significant in featuring *The Nation*, which, in addition to political developments of the time, proved to be an important vehicle in the realisation of an Irish national identity.

James Mahony (1810-79)

QUEEN VICTORIA AND PRINCE ALBERT OPENING THE 1853 DUBLIN GREAT EXHIBITION 1853

Watercolour on paper, 60.1 x 73.3 cm NGI NO. 2453

IN 1853, during the period when Irish people countrywide were still seeking to come to terms with the Great Famine of 1845-50, an impressive exhibition of art and industry was held in Dublin. The display, largely financed by William Dargan (who had made his fortune as a builder of railways), was organised by the Irish Industrial Exhibition Committee. The event was held in a specially constructed temporary building of glass, iron and wood on the lawn of Leinster House, at that time the residence of the Royal Dublin Society. Its design was based on the Crystal Palace, created by Joseph Paxton for a similar exhibition held in Hyde Park, London, in 1851. The Dublin 'Crystal Palace' was designed by the Sligo-born architect, John Benson. It covered six and a half acres in total, and the great Hall, shown in James Mahony's watercolour, was 129.5 metres (425 feet) long, 30 metres (100 feet) wide and 32 metres (105 feet) high. On display was a huge range of industrial, scientific and cultural exhibits. The Fine Art section of the exhibition was particularly well received and the interest it aroused led to pressure being put on the Parliament in London to establish a permanent Gallery of Painters, Sculptures and Fine Arts in Dublin. Eleven years later the National Gallery of Ireland opened its doors to the public in a new building located on the spot where the exhibition had taken place.

James Mahony came from Cork, and much of his career was spent as an illustrator for English magazines. In Ireland, he is well known for his magnificent panorama of Dublin, as well as his series of watercolours recording the visit of Queen Victoria and Prince Albert in 1853. The present picture shows the royal couple about to open the exhibition in the Great Hall. They are followed by their young sons, Arthur and Albert. In the right foreground of the picture can be seen the executive committee who organised the event, as they wait to be presented to their Royal Highnesses. Standing in conversation at the left of the picture is William Dargan, who financed the exhibition. Mahony's eye for detail is breathtaking. With wonderful precision he delineates the complex design of the roof and the vast throngs of people attending the opening. Some of the fine art exhibits are also depicted, among them a large equestrian statue of Queen Victoria by the sculptor Baron Marochetti. This centrally placed statue would have served to underline the political unity between England and Ireland at the time.

Erskine Nicol (1825-1904)

AN EJECTED FAMILY 1853

Oil on canvas,
50 x 82 cm
NGI NO. 4577

DURING THE mid nineteenth century in Ireland there were remarkably few paintings documenting contemporary horrific events such as the Famine, evictions and emigration. *An Ejected Family*, painted in 1853, is one of the few surviving pictures that reflects the horror of events in poverty-stricken Ireland. The scene illustrated here shows the deep despair of a young labourer as he looks at the cottage from which he and his family have been evicted. The reason for the eviction is that they could not pay the rent. The failure of the potato crop, due to a fungus brought on by bad weather, caused widespread poverty and starvation, as it was the main source of food. There is another image of the failure of the potato crop by Daniel McDonald (1847) and an eviction scene painted by Lady Elizabeth Butler (1890) in the Collection of the Folklore Department, University College Dublin. In the National Gallery's painting, the man is surrounded by his family: his wife looks to her husband, baby in arms, face full of worry and concern for their future; two of their children lie on a grass bank watching their cattle being taken by the bailiff; the elderly grandfather rests his hand on the man's shoulder, as if in silent support; meanwhile, close by, a child looks innocently at her family, totally bewildered at the scene taking place. The young labourer is depicted as a stereotypical Irishman, in breeches, long coat and hat. Nicol skilfully heightens the tension by including a heavy, downcast sky that augurs bad weather and echoes the mood of the scene. Before the Famine, many people lived in mud cabins such as the one shown here. Magazines like *The London Illustrated News* dispatched artists into the most distressed areas to produce illustrations to accompany their correspondents' reports. Most Irish artists were reluctant to exhibit pictures that documented the horror of contemporary events because political statements would be viewed as criticism of the ruling British Government, and they were also unlikely to find buyers for such subject matter. *An Ejected Family*, painted by a Scottish artist, succeeded because it was presented in the manner of an emotional stage-Irish scene when it was shown in 1854 at the Royal Scottish Academy.

Born in Leith, Scotland, in 1825, Erskine Nicol studied art at the Trustees' Academy, Edinburgh, where his teachers included Sir William Allen and Thomas Duncan. He worked for some time as a drawing master at Leith Academy before moving to Ireland for a four-year period (1846-50), where he received a teaching appointment from the Department of Science and Art in Dublin. The pictures that Nicol painted during his Irish stay explore the social life of the country, often in a humorous, satirical manner. Most of his Irish subject pictures, however, were painted on his return to Scotland. In executing these works, he employed more caricature and satire than in his portrayal of similar Scottish peasant themes. While his pictures are meticulously composed and painted, many of the Irish characters seem overly theatrical. Nicol was elected an associate of the Royal Scottish Academy in 1855, and was made an academician in 1859. He moved to London in 1863 and was elected an associate of the Royal Academy in 1868. He retired in 1885 and died in 1904.

Edwin Hayes (1820-1904)

AN EMIGRANT SHIP, DUBLIN BAY, SUNSET 1853

Oil on canvas,
58 x 86 cm
NGI NO. 1209

EDWIN HAYES, though born in Bristol, came to Ireland when he was young. He studied at the Dublin Society Schools and decided that he would become a marine painter. In order to learn about the sea, he sailed around the Irish coast in a yacht and later took a job on a ship bound for America, experiences that served him well in his artistic career. For a time he was apprenticed to an artist called Telbin. Between 1842 and 1852 he lived in Dublin. He began exhibiting at the Royal Hibernian Academy in 1852, a practice he continued right up to the year of his death in 1904. In 1852 he moved to London and worked as a scene painter. In 1854 he started exhibiting at the British Institution in London, and the following year he showed at the Royal Academy, where he contributed to successive exhibitions, becoming an academician in 1863. He travelled extensively, visiting France, Spain and Italy. Hayes seems to have returned to Ireland regularly, showing Irish subjects at the RHA, of which he was made a full member in 1871. Although he painted mainly in oils, his marine watercolours also display true feeling for the power of the sea, sky and sailing boats.

An Emigrant Ship, Dublin Bay, dated 1853, is significant because it is one of the few surviving oil paintings that represent an episode in Irish history dealing with mass emigration. The picture illustrates boatloads of destitute emigrants being rowed to a large sailing vessel, the identity of which is unknown, anchored at the mouth of the river Liffey. Although by 1850 the worst of the Great Famine had passed, the country did not recover from the catastrophe for many decades. The people depicted on the boat are emigrating to seek a new life in England, the United States or Canada. There is a note of hope in *An Emigrant Ship*, represented by a dramatic, flaming sunset, which is Hayes' way of anticipating a better future for its migrant passengers. The population of Ireland in 1851 was approximately 6.1 million, having fallen by two million during the Great Famine, with almost a million dying from starvation, cold and disease, while another million emigrated. The choice was bleak, between death and emigration, with the result that hundreds of thousands of people fled from the country in order to survive. Circumstances on many of the ships were appalling, resulting in people arriving often diseased and needing attention. Emigration continued after the Famine and by 1901 the population was reduced to about 4.6 million. While Hayes' picture is a poignant record of this tragic period, it must be remembered that emigration represented the only option for many of the population.

Michael Angelo Hayes (1820-77)

SACKVILLE STREET, DUBLIN c.1853

Watercolour with
gum arabic and
white highlights on
paper,
54.5 x 77.6 cm
NGI NO. 2980

Sackville street (now O'Connell Street), painted by Michael Angelo Hayes in the early
1850s, depicts Dublin's main thoroughfare. It was renamed O'Connell Street in 1924,
after Daniel O'Connell the statesman, whose statue, designed by John Henry Foley and
erected in 1882, dominates the south end of the street. The view shows several important
landmarks, beginning with the portico of the General Post Office. Commissioned in 1814,
and designed by Francis Johnston, who supervised its construction in 1818, it was damaged
during the Easter Rising of 1916 and rebuilt in 1929. It was here that the Proclamation of
Independence was read out by Patrick Pearse. Directly across from this building was the
large, classically inspired Imperial Hotel. This was bought in 1902 by Clery & Company
and demolished in the 1920s to make way for the present store. In the distance the spire of
St George's Church, Hardwicke Place, can be seen. Dominating the street is the tall landmark, Nelson's Pillar. Over 40 metres (134 feet) high, this famous monument was erected
in 1808 and provided a sculptural focal point for the long, wide street. The statue commemorating Admiral Lord Nelson was carved by Thomas Kirk (1781-1845), who was also
responsible for the statues of Hibernia, Mercury and Fidelity over the General Post Office.
The Pillar was partially destroyed by an explosion in 1966, the year marking the fiftieth
anniversary of the Easter Rising, and demolished by army engineers two days later. The
scene offers a fascinating glimpse not only of how the street looked in the 1850s, but also
of Dublin city life: people stroll on the sidewalks, various carriages and carts make their
way up and down the thoroughfare, and an omnibus can be glimpsed parked at the Pillar.

The parents of this artist, in naming him as they did, clearly had ambitions for their
son to become an artist! He was born in Waterford and trained with his father, Edward
Hayes, who was a portrait painter in watercolour. A talented draughtsman, the younger
Hayes had drawings entitled *Car-Travelling in the South of Ireland* published in London when
he was only sixteen. He specialised as a painter of horses and military subjects. In 1842 he
was appointed military painter-in-ordinary to the lord lieutenant. He spent the next few
years in London, where he exhibited watercolours, and in 1848 he was elected an associate
of the prestigious Society of Painters in Watercolour. On his return to Dublin he was
elected an associate of the Royal Hibernian Academy in 1853 and became a member one year
later. He proved to be highly controversial in his involvement with the administrative affairs
of the Academy. Hayes painted in oils but was also a very accomplished watercolourist.

Daniel Maclise (1806-70)

THE MARRIAGE OF PRINCESS AOIFE WITH STRONGBOW 1854

Oil on canvas,
309 x 505 cm
NGI NO. 205

The Marriage of Princess Aoife with Strongbow, one of Maclise's most masterful paintings, was exhibited at the Royal Academy, London, in 1854. The picture narrates the historic episode when the Normans, who had settled in England, were provided with the opportunity to invade Ireland. This was given to them by Dermot McMurrough, the king of Leinster, who had been expelled from his kingdom and had gone to seek assistance from the Norman leader, Richard de Clare, known as Strongbow. In return for his help, McMurrough promised Strongbow the hand of his daughter Aoife in marriage, and after his death that he would become king of Leinster. In May 1169, the Normans besieged the town of Wexford, and the following year Strongbow himself arrived and captured Waterford. Maclise's painting depicts the wedding of Strongbow and Aoife on the battlefield near Waterford, which later generations saw as sealing the union between England and Ireland. Maclise relates this particular event to the passing of Gaelic Ireland and the arrival of a foreign force. The wedding takes place in front of a ruined church and a round tower. Details such as the gold torcs, dating from the Bronze Age, worn by the defeated warriors, and the broken strings of the old bard's harp – all symbolise the death of a proud Celtic heritage (although anachronistic for the twelfth century). Prior to designing the picture, the artist consulted his Irish antiquarian friends in an attempt to ensure that details of costume and weaponry were correct. It is significant that Maclise presents the conquered Irish as a noble ancient race, dignified in their defeat, whereas the Normans are shown as a dark, impressive force insensitive to Irish customs, illustrated by Strongbow placing his foot on a high cross. It is possible that in portraying this event as a sacrifice, symbolised by Aoife, to the powerful Norman soldier Strongbow, Maclise intended the picture to reflect on the recent unsuccessful 1848 Young Irelander rebellion and the 1845-50 Famine. The picture, with its romantic, nationalistic sympathies, alludes to the long history of foreign oppression of Ireland. An extremely accomplished, ambitious work in scale, design and execution, it serves as an apt testament that Maclise was one of the most successful history painters of his day.

Maclise was a Cork-born artist, who worked in a bank before enrolling at the Academy of Plaster Casts in Cork. He lived by making portrait drawings, and as a result of an early sketch made in Cork of Sir Walter Scott, he was encouraged to pursue his chosen career. He moved to London in 1827, where he established himself as a portraitist and illustrator, gradually turning to history painting. A bookish man, he loved to research subjects and enjoyed moving in literary circles, including that of William M. Thackeray and Charles Dickens. In 1844 he was one of six artists chosen to decorate the new Houses of Parliament in London. The murals he executed for Westminster between 1858 and 1865 represent the high point of a remarkably successful career.

Edward Murphy (c.1796-1841)

PAROQUETS c.1861

Oil on canvas,
85 x 61 cm
NGI NO. 161

Lttle is known about the accomplished artist who painted this work. Edward Murphy studied at the Royal Dublin Society's School, where he was a successful pupil. He taught for some time, while also doing caricatures for a Dublin publisher. For many years he concentrated on still-life and flower painting in the manner of seventeenth-century Dutch artists. This kind of subject matter was popular with nineteenth-century Irish artists and was enjoyed by the art-buying public, who liked to decorate the walls of their homes with such scenes. Murphy exhibited his work, which included an occasional landscape painting, at various exhibitions. Sadly, this gifted artist took his own life in 1841.

Paroquets is a decorative painting of birds, which depicts a white and a brilliantly coloured paroquet, with a green parrot perched on the boughs of a tree. One of the birds is anchored to a branch by a length of rope. All three are framed within a large stone arch garlanded with creeping ivy. The birds are positioned to form a pyramidal composition. Silhouetted against the backdrop of sky and cloud, they create a dramatic and eye-catching picture. The artist's palette relies on a vivid use of primary colours. This may be why it is so popular with younger audiences. Bright colours are seen in the deep blue and red of the most colourful of the birds and repeated in the painting of the sky and in the beak and neck area of the smaller green parrot. The pink coxcomb of the white bird is picked up in the flowering branches beneath. This interesting juxtaposition of colour helps to unite the whole composition in a visually exciting way. The painting of the feathers is especially skilful, while the modelling of light on the feathers of the white paroquet is masterly. All these diverse elements combine to create a superb, attractive painting.

Thomas Farrell (1827-1900)

WILLIAM DARGAN (1799-1867) 1863

Bronze,
258.5 cm ht.
NGI NO. 8277

THIS IS A portrait bronze of William Dargan, the Irish railway magnate. Dargan is known as the man who built the first Irish railroad, the Dublin–Kingstown (now Dún Laoghaire) line, on which the trains first travelled from Westland Row (now Pearse Street station) on 17 December 1838. He continued to construct a series of important railroads, including the Ulster Railway Line, opened in August 1839, and the Great Southern and Western Railway (1843-50). He also built the Ulster Canal (1834-42). Like many other wealthy Victorian businessmen, Dargan believed that it was a duty to bring the arts to the public. In 1853 an art and industries exhibition was held in Dublin. It derived from a similar exhibition held in London two years earlier at the Crystal Palace. Much of the funding for this enterprise came from Dargan. At the close of the exhibition, a committee was formed which decided that an Irish National Gallery would be a suitable testimonial for the railway magnate's generosity. When the National Gallery of Ireland first opened its doors in 1864, the bronze statue by Thomas Farrell was in place in the forecourt of the building.

Dressed simply in a frock-coat, thrown open, and waistcoat and trousers, Dargan stands in a relaxed pose against the granite plinth. He leans on his left arm while the fingers of the right hand are passed in between the buttons of the waistcoat. His left foot and leg are thrown forward and the weight of the figure is sustained by the right leg. The head, turned slightly, and the expression on the face suggest a reflective and thoughtful subject. The treatment of the drapery, which details the soft folds of the materials, gives a sense of energy and vigor to the otherwise inert figure, while creating a soft, natural outline to the modelled form.

The statue, a convincing likeness of Dargan, is a fine example of the work of the sculptor Thomas Farrell. Farrell entered the Modelling School of the Royal Dublin Society in 1843, and by 1849 he was exhibiting with the Royal Hibernian Academy. For many years he had a lucrative practice. In his statues and busts he was successful in capturing the characteristic features of his subjects, and his best works, of which this is one, are well posed and strongly modelled.

Matthew Lawless (1837-64)

THE SICK CALL c.1863

Oil on canvas,
63 x 103 cm
NGI NO. 864

The Sick Call was exhibited at the Royal Academy in 1863, the year before Lawless died. The full title is: *'A Sick Call: Is any man sick among you? Let him bring the priests of the Church, and let them pray over him, anointing him with oil in the Name of the Lord'* (James 5:14). The theme may be a reflection on the artist's own ill-health and his strong religious beliefs. The scene depicts a priest crossing a river in order to render the Last Rites to a dying person. He is accompanied by three white-robed acolytes and a weeping woman, who has clearly fetched him, and a young boy, possibly her son. The acolytes and the boy reflect the vitality of youth and relieve some of the solemnity of this work. It has been suggested that the model for the priest was Sir Benjamin Ward Richardson, a well-known London physician who was attached to the Royal Infirmary for Diseases in 1856. He would have been a most suitable model if, indeed, he was Lawless' doctor, as has been suggested. The background shows a small town with red tiled roofs, distinctive towers and church spires. A memoir written in 1898 indicates that the architectural setting was inspired by a view of the city of Prague, although it appears closer in mood to the medieval Belgian city of Bruges. A popular work when exhibited in Manchester in 1887, it continues to be much admired by the public in the National Gallery of Ireland.

Matthew James Lawless was born in Dublin, the son of a wealthy solicitor. His family moved to London in 1845 and he went to school near Bath. He began his artistic training under Francis Stephen Cary and James Matthew Leith, and after attending Langham School he completed his training with the Irish artist Henry O'Neill. He enjoyed reasonable success as a painter and illustrator. Between 1858 and 1863 he exhibited narrative genre scenes at the Royal Academy, influenced by the French painters Meissonier, Gerome, Tissot, Couture and Delaroche. He met Meissonier in 1860 in Paris and his technique owes a great deal to Meissonier's finely executed panel paintings. Apart from the work he did as an illustrator, *The Sick Call* (which was engraved for the *Illustrated London News*) is the only known painting by Lawless upon which to judge his work. His short life was plagued by illness and he died at the age of twenty-seven.

Frederic William Burton (1816-1900)

THE MEETING ON THE TURRET STAIRS 1864

Watercolour on
paper,
95.5 x 60.8 cm
NGI NO. 2358

The Meeting on the Turret Stairs, painted by Burton in 1864, is considered by many to be his masterpiece, and perhaps the most famous of Irish watercolours. The picture, also known as *Hellelil and Hildebrand*, illustrates an episode from a Danish ballad translated by Whitley Stokes and published in *Fraser's Magazine* of 1855. It is in keeping with literary and medieval themes much used by English Pre-Raphaelite artists. The story tells of Hellelil, who falls in love with Hildebrand, the Prince of Engellend. He was one of her bodyguards. Her father did not approve and ordered his sons to kill him. The drama ends with Hildebrand, having slain seven of Hellelil's brothers, dying at the hand of the youngest. Burton chose to depict the final meeting of the lovers. On the steps close by can be seen a fading rose, symbolising the tragic event to follow. Burton executed numerous preparatory studies for this work, several of which are in the National Gallery of Ireland's Collection. He worked slowly and meticulously on the picture, using fine brushstrokes reminiscent of his miniature technique, building up depth of colour and using opaque gouache to highlight individual details. The writer and poet George Eliot (the pen name of Mary Ann Evans, 1819-80) wrote to Burton: 'the subject might have been the most vulgar thing in the world, the artist has raised it to the highest pitch of emotion'.

Following Frederic Burton's early career as a miniaturist and illustrator of Irish subject pictures, he spent some time in Germany, between 1851 and 1857, at the invitation of Maximilian II of Bavaria, to curate the royal collection. It was an important time for the artist, who copied old master paintings, sketched landscapes and figure studies, and was particularly influenced by Nazarene and German romantic painting. He kept in frequent contact with Ireland, returning often to see family and old friends. His Irish landscapes of this period are exceptional and place him in the forefront of watercolourists in this genre. In 1858 Burton settled in London, becoming part of the Rossetti Pre-Raphaelite circle, but not a member of their movement. He gave up painting following his appointment as Director of the National Gallery, London, in 1874, where he is chiefly remembered for reorganising the Collection and for the outstanding acquisitions he made for the Gallery. He was knighted in 1884 and retired in 1894. Although unmarried, he cared for the family of his brother who had died young. The artist is buried in Mount Jerome Cemetery in Dublin.

John Henry Foley (1818-74)

EQUESTRIAN STATUE OF QUEEN VICTORIA (1819-1901) 1865

Bronze,
44 cm ht.
NGI NO. 8251

THIS IS an unusually lively, appealing portrayal of the forty-six-year-old Queen Victoria. Statues and monuments traditionally associated with this royal personage are frequently heavy and baroque, with the queen shown as a serious, ponderous and unsmiling figure. This bronze equestrian statuette portrays an active Queen Victoria, with all the elegance and artistry traditionally associated with John Henry Foley's sculpture. Riding side-saddle, she is shown in a rather formal pose, which suggests that the occasion is ceremonial. She wears a bonnet and long flowing gown, which falls in heavy folds, and holds the reins of the high-stepping horse. She appears to have full control of the animal. The sculptor cleverly conveys this by contrasting the poised, erect figure of the monarch with the more lively, restless stance of the horse.

Victoria ruled as Queen of the United Kingdom of Great Britain and Ireland (1837-1901) and Empress of India (1876-1901). She married Albert in 1840. In the course of her reign she visited Ireland on four occasions. During the Famine of 1845-50, she contributed £2,000 to the British Relief Association. While she enjoyed walking and riding during her visits to Ireland, she preferred to holiday in the Scottish Highlands, where she had a residence at Balmoral built to Albert's design. She urged strong government during the Land War, and remained unimpressed with Charles Stewart Parnell and the Irish Parliamentary Party.

John Henry Foley was recognised as the finest sculptor of his day in England. He was considered significant enough to be chosen to carve the statue of Prince Albert for the Albert Memorial in London. He had trained alongside his brother Edward at the Dublin Society Schools, where he won many prizes before going to London and the Royal Academy Schools. His talent was recognised early in his career and he was employed on statues for the new Houses of Parliament in London in the early 1840s. He enjoyed a highly successful career and received many commissions for both portrait busts and public statuary. His best-known Irish works are the Father Mathew statue in Cork city, the statues of Edmund Burke and Oliver Goldsmith outside Trinity College Dublin, and the Daniel O'Connell monument in O'Connell Street, Dublin, which he designed in 1867 but did not live to see erected in 1882. Foley was a slow worker, who altered and refined each piece as he worked on it. His sculpture is noted for its precision of detail and sensitivity to the subject. This small work, created to celebrate and inspire pride and loyalty in young Queen Victoria, is impressive. The bronze equestrian sculpture combines the distance and dignity required of the subject with an accessible and affectionate monument to the reigning queen.

Nathaniel Hone the Younger (1831-1917)

THE CLIFFS AT ETRETAT, NORMANDY c.1867

Oil on canvas,
61 x 92 cm
NGI NO. 1429

IN THE LATE 1860s Nathaniel Hone the Younger began to visit Normandy and Brittany, where he was much taken by Etretat, a fishing village with stunning white cliffs some twenty-five kilometres north-west of Le Havre on the north-west coast of France. Etretat was notable for its unchanged pattern of traditional life, which made it a most desirable location for painters. During the late 1860s the area, with its attractive coastal scenery and beaches, was beginning to be discovered by artists such as Courbet and Monet. Prior to painting this picture, Hone did a number of preliminary studies, which illustrate the stages the artist worked through before arriving at his final exhibition piece. The canvas is based on direct observation of nature; it reflects *plein-air* painting and the influence of the Barbizon school of painters. It is a busy composition, with lots of activity. Boats have been pulled on to the beach, fishermen young and old repair their nets, and a woman sits to one side observing the scene. The picture was titled *Beach, Etretat* when Hone exhibited it at the Royal Hibernian Academy in 1883; however, by 1911, when he showed it at the Loan Exhibition in Belfast, he had given it the title *Etretat Forty Years Ago*.

Hone was one of the most important and influential landscape painters among Irish artists of the late nineteenth and early twentieth century. The grand-nephew of Nathaniel Hone the Elder (1718-84), he was born into a wealthy Dublin family, and after graduating from Trinity College, he began work as an engineer on the railways. However, he changed his mind about his career, and in 1853 went to Paris to study art. This signified a new departure for Irish artists, who had previously looked to England for training. Hone marks the beginning of a trend to train on the Continent, travelling to established art schools in Antwerp and Paris before going on to paint in Fontainebleau and Brittany. About 1857 Hone settled in Barbizon, a small village beside the forest of Fontainebleau, then much frequented by French artists who enjoyed landscape painting and who could live fairly cheaply in the locality. For most of his time in France he lived in Fontainebleau or Barbizon. There he met many prominent artists, including Corot, Harpignies, Millet and Rousseau. In 1872, aged forty, after seventeen years working in France, Hone returned to Ireland. His absorption with nature and the changing light, which characterises his French works, continued to be a feature of his later Irish landscapes and coastal scenes.

Andrew Nicholl (1804-86)

A VIEW OF THE RIVER FOYLE AND CITY OF DERRY THROUGH A BANK OF FLOWERS 1870

Watercolour on
paper,
35.3 x 52.2 cm
NGI no. 7769

ANDREW NICHOLL was born in Belfast, where he was apprenticed to a local printer for seven years. During this time he produced a series of 113 watercolour views of the Antrim coast (purchased by the Ulster Museum, Belfast, in 1957). His early style, evident in hard-edged pencil outlines, clear fresh washes and stylised compositions, developed after visiting London, where he became familiar with the work of Cuyp, De Wint and Copley Fielding. It must have been about this time that he saw works by Turner, who became a major influence throughout his career. Nicholl moved to Dublin in 1832, where he seems to have devised his most attractive compositions, comprising distant views seen through banks of wild flowers. At this time he began exhibiting at the Royal Hibernian Academy. In 1836 he and his brother William were founder members of the Belfast Association of Artists. For fourteen years Nicholl toured Ireland, providing topograpical views for engravings. Between 1845 and 1849 he is recorded as having travelled to Ceylon, where he taught drawing at the Colombo Academy. He returned to London in 1849/50 and divided his time between Dublin, Belfast and London, where he died in 1886.

This is one of a number of watercolours by Nicholl illustrating a view of the city of Derry, seen through a border of flowers. The view depicts, on the right, the Church of All Saints, with the Carlisle bridge in the centre spanning the river Foyle, while the Cathedral Church of St Colum can be seen on the left side dominating the old city of Derry. The picture is signed on the bottom right 'A. Nicholl RHA'. The border of flowers is startling in its clarity and freshness and includes crisply painted blue and red poppies, cornflowers, forget-me-nots and foxgloves. The delicate white sprays of cow-parsley were drawn with the tip of a sharp knife, which scraped away the darker paint, exposing the white paper underneath, a technique clearly influenced by Turner. The scale of the flowers is huge in comparison to the landscape, which is minutely observed. Other similar views by this artist include Bray, Co. Wicklow, and Carrickfergus and Portrush, Co. Antrim. Nicholl's flower pieces are among the most beautiful and memorable watercolours Ireland has ever produced.

Sarah Purser (1848-1943)

LE PETIT DÉJEUNER 1881

Oil on canvas,
35 x 27 cm
NGI NO. 1424

THE SUBJECT of *Le Petit Déjeuner* is the dancer Maria Feller, the daughter of an Italian count and a dancer. Feller was a voice and music student with Gaetano Brega in Paris, and for a period she shared the apartment at 40 Avenue des Ternes with Purser, and two Swiss artists, Louise Breslau and Sophie Schoppi. This portrait was executed during the summer of 1881, at a time when Feller was teaching music. It was first entitled *This Also is Vanity* before it acquired its present title, *Le Petit Déjeuner*, in 1909. It is more of an informal portrait in the relaxed way in which it conveys something of the ambience of Paris in the 1880s, with people passing idle hours chatting in cafés. Although both Bastien-Lepage and Degas had an influence on Purser's work, the informal pose and photo-like compositions of the picture are closer to Degas. Feller is shown seated on a bentwood chair wearing an outdoor dress, a green-grey jacket with a white lace jabot, blue skirt and brown bonnet tied with white ribbons. Although full of detail, nothing in the picture distracts the viewer's attention away from the singer's moody and pensive expression. Purser regarded this picture highly and was very selective about where it was exhibited.

Sarah Purser was one of the most important women in the development of Irish twentieth-century art. She came from a wealthy family, and had already begun to train as an artist when her father's business collapsed. She may have studied at the Dublin Society Schools (renamed the Metropolitan School of Art in 1877) before moving to Paris in 1878 to study at the Académie Julian. As there was no private income for her to draw upon, Purser endured considerable hardship in Paris. On her return to Dublin she determined to establish herself as a portrait painter, and became one of the most successful and wealthy portraitists of her generation. She became involved in numerous cultural activities of the period, in addition to holding a successful, major loan exhibition of modern paintings and showing the works of John Butler Yeats and Nathaniel Hone the Younger. With Edward Martyn (1859-1924), a writer and leading figure in Irish cultural affairs, she established An Túr Gloine, a co-operative stained-glass workshop (1903-43). She also founded an art history scholarship with her cousin, Senator John Griffith, which is in existence to this very day. She was one of the driving forces behind the Municipal Gallery of Modern Art and the Friends of the National Collections. An unfailingly energetic and enthusiastic woman, she continued to paint well into her eighties.

Henry Jones Thaddeus (1859-1929)

THE WOUNDED POACHER c.1881

Oil on canvas,
120 x 85 cm
NGI NO. 4487

HENRY THADDEUS JONES was born in Cork, but after he established himself as a portraitist, he inverted his name to H. Jones Thaddeus. He attended the Cork School of Art and won prizes from the Royal Dublin Society, enabling him to study at Heatherley's Academy in London between 1879 and 1880. He went to Paris in 1880, where he was taught at the Académie Julian by Lefebvre and Boulanger, and in 1881 he visited Brittany, settling in Concarneau. He came back to Paris in 1882, travelling on to Florence via Moret-sur-Loing in the forest of Fontainebleau, before returning to London three years later. While Thaddeus concentrated on portraiture for his livelihood, he also executed genre scenes and occasional landscapes. Between 1886 and 1902 he exhibited at the Royal Hibernian Academy, the main body of his work being portraits. He travelled throughout Europe, visiting Australia and the Middle East, and also spending time in North Africa and the United States. His autobiography, *Recollections of a Court Painter*, was published in 1912. Thaddeus felt his greatest distinction to be his portraits of two popes: Leo XIII, painted in 1885, and another version in 1899, and Pius X in 1903. He exhibited his portrait of Pope Leo XIII in 1901 at the RHA, where it was justifiably celebrated, resulting in the artist being made a full member of the Academy that year.

Le Retour du Bracconie Irlande, known in English as *The Wounded Poacher*, was accepted at the Paris Salon in 1881. It was noticed by Albert Wolff, the art critic of *Le Figaro*, who recognised that the twenty-two-year-old had exceptional talent. It is an ambitious picture, intended to show off his abilities. The wounded poacher is placed in a dark cabin where his injuries are attended to by an attractive young woman, who is more than likely his wife. The weather-beaten figure of the man contrasts with the soft, warm figure of the concerned woman. He appears like a wounded soldier returned from war and she takes on the calm pose of a ministering nurse. The manner in which a chair has been overturned, and the poacher's hat, gun and two rabbits have been dropped on the floor, suggests the drama of the moment. By including hanging nets, a basket of cabbages and carrots, and the worn hearth, he reveals the simple lifestyle of the cabin's inhabitants. A beautifully executed canvas, it is also a superb example of contemporary realism.

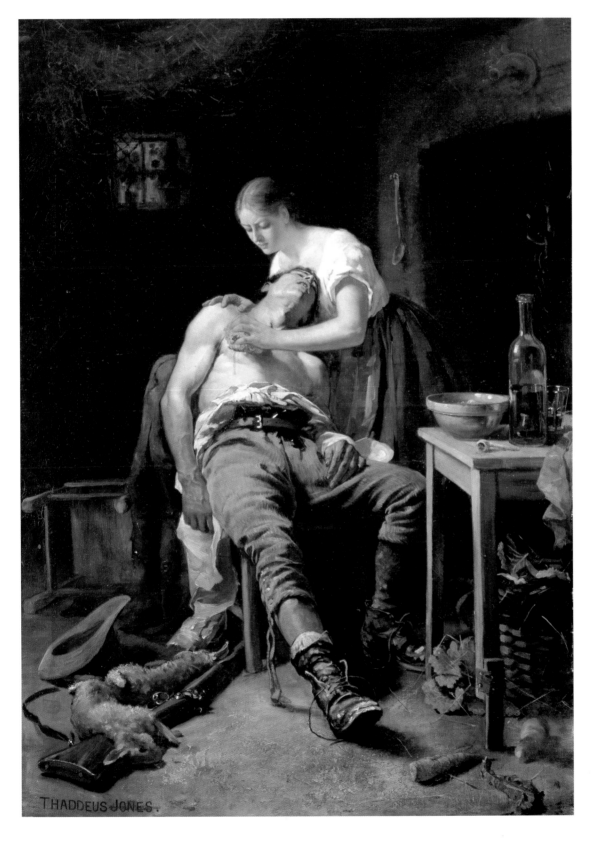

THADDEUS JONES.

Joseph Malachy Kavanagh (1856-1918)

OLD CONVENT GATE, DINAN 1883

Oil on canvas,
56 x 38 cm
NGI NO. 1194

JOSEPH MALACHY KAVANAGH, a Dublin-born artist, was nineteen when his work was first accepted by the Royal Hibernian Academy and he won a silver medal at the Royal Dublin Society the same year. Walter Osborne was a friend of Kavanagh and they both attended the Dublin Metropolitan School of Art and the RHA Schools. Kavanagh, along with Osborne and Nathaniel Hill, went to Belgium to study at Antwerp in 1881. The three students spent most of their time in Verlat's life class at the Antwerp Academy. From 1883 to 1887 he worked in Brittany and Normandy, exhibiting French scenes at the RHA for a number of years before returning to Ireland in 1887. Kavanagh became very interested in etching and in 1890 the Dublin Art Club issued a portfolio which included five of his etchings. He taught at the RHA schools, took a keen interest in Academy affairs, and in 1910 he was appointed Keeper of the RHA. He was deeply affected when the RHA building in Abbey Street was burnt down in 1916. Two years later he died in Dublin.

During 1883, when Kavanagh and Osborne were in Brittany, they visited Dinan. The *Old Convent Gate, Dinan* is very close in composition and style to Osborne's *Beneath St Jacques, Antwerp*. Kavanagh was particularly good at illustrating architectural subjects and interested in drawing street scenes, for which he frequently used preliminary drawings. This picture reflects the influence of his period of study in Antwerp. Painted in Belgium, it has an affinity to Dutch realism of the late nineteenth century. Kavanagh found it difficult to depict figures, and often, as in the case of the *Old Convent Gate*, he represented people from behind. He was clearly influenced by French *plein-air* painting, but ignored contemporary impressionist painting. Kavanagh was one of the finest academic landscape and seascape painters of his time, with an ability to render transient light and weather effects. His output included oils, watercolours, drawings and etchings. His works reflect quiet, peaceful scenes, such as his views of the suburbs and landscape of Co. Dublin. Many too evoke a still, moody atmosphere, notably in his paintings of the Dublin coastline.

John Hughes (1865-1941)

SIR FREDERIC WILLIAM BURTON (1816-1900) 1890s

Marble,
18.7 cm ht.
NGI NO. 8134

THIS UNUSUAL sculpture in marble, depicting Sir Frederic William Burton, is after a plaster life mask. The process of making a life or death mask involves the use of plaster-of-Paris, which is moulded over the face, already oiled or thinly waxed. Tubes are inserted into the nostrils and ears to keep them clear (in the case of the life mask, this allows the sitter to breathe comfortably). The plaster takes an imprint of the face, thus providing the most accurate record of the features. In ancient times the Egyptians made death masks with thin, gold plates, and the Romans made them with wax. The aim of such a procedure is that it enables a sculptor to carve or model a most convincing likeness of a figure. In the case of Sir Frederic William Burton, this method permitted the sculptor, John Hughes, to carve in marble an accurate likeness from a life mask taken about 1850. Burton was a watercolour artist, who is not known to have ever exhibited or painted in oils. Considered a brilliant technician in the medium, he produced works of great feeling and refinement of colour. An art historian and antiquary, he was a founding member of the Archaeological Society of Ireland, and a Fellow of the Royal Society of Antiquaries of Ireland. Through his association with Lady Gregory he became one of the first guarantors of the Irish Literary Theatre. From 1874 to 1894 he was Director of the National Gallery, London. He is buried in Mount Jerome Cemetery in Dublin.

John Hughes was one of Ireland's most talented and accomplished sculptors working at the turn of the century. In 1880 he enrolled as a full-time student at the Dublin Metropolitan School of Art, and as a scholarship student attended the National Art Training School at South Kensington, London, in 1890. He visited Paris and Italy, where he was deeply influenced by Italian Renaissance sculptors such as Donatello and Michelangelo. Hughes returned to teach at the Metropolitan Art School in 1894, at the same time undertaking commissioned work. His most important commissions include an elaborate monument to Queen Victoria, a carved Madonna and Child, and a bronze relief of the dead Christ for St Brendan's Cathedral, Loughrea, Co. Galway. His reputation for achieving a convincing likeness of his sitters is borne out by his many commissions for busts and full-length statuary.

Richard Thomas Moynan (1856-1906)

MILITARY MANOEUVRES 1891

Oil on canvas,
148 x 240 cm
NGI NO. 4364

*M*ilitary Manoeuvres is a narrative picture, humorous in mood, for the manoeuvres referred to are those of children pretending to be a regimental band, parading in front of a trooper and his girlfriend. The scene is considered to be set in the main street of Leixlip village in Co. Kildare. The trooper has been identified as a member of the Fourth Royal Irish Dragoon Guards, a regiment based in Ireland during the 1880s. He wears the walking-out uniform of the cavalry regiment, and notices that the leader of the children's group is wearing the regimental band helmet. His fashionably dressed girlfriend tries to make him see the joke. The children are dressed in ragged, patched clothes; most of them are barefooted and only two are wearing boots. Their musical instruments are ordinary household objects, pots and pans, tin boxes, buckets and saucepan lids. Three girls watch the scene from the pavement, and one, in the left foreground, dressed in a traditional costume, carries a basket of ferns. The children have fun trying to tease the soldier, and much to his annoyance everyone in the town stops to watch. *Military Manoeuvres* is one of a number of beautifully painted subject pictures by Moynan. Some preliminary drawings exist, revealing how he worked out his ideas towards the final composition. This picture has all the hallmarks of a good story because it engages the viewer's full attention in every element of the scene.

Richard Thomas Moynan was born in Dublin. He first studied medicine at the Royal College of Surgeons but then decided to train as an artist. His early training was at the Dublin Metropolitan School of Art, followed by the Royal Hibernian Academy School, where in 1883 he was awarded the Albert Prize. In the same year he went abroad with Roderic O'Conor to Antwerp, where he attended life classes under Charles Verlat, and in 1884 he won first prize for life painting. He moved to Paris in 1884, where he remained until 1886, when he returned to Ireland. He developed his reputation as a portrait painter, although his strength lay in genre subject pictures, depicting scenes of everyday life, such as *Military Manoeuvres*. Moynan frequently chose to paint children engaged in everyday activities or wistful reverie. Often his pictures showed humorous incidents and many of his works demonstrated a sympathy towards the poor.

Richard Barter (c.1824-96)

CHARLES STEWART PARNELL, MP (1846-91), STATESMAN 1893

Bronze,
33 cm ht.
NGI NO. 8086

THIS PORTRAIT BUST of Charles Stewart Parnell was executed two years after his death by the sculptor Richard Barter. It is one of a number of portraits of Parnell in a variety of media owned by the National Gallery of Ireland. In spite of having been modelled from photographs, it nevertheless vividly conveys an excellent physical likeness of the man, as well as a strong sense of character. Parnell's distinctive bearded face, with its high forehead and cheekbones, is immediately recognisable. The upright cast of the head indicates a proud nature. The determination to succeed, regardless of the odds, is captured by the artist in the steady, purposeful glance, as is the sense of detached aloofness for which he was also renowned.

Charles Stewart Parnell was born in Avondale, Co. Wicklow, in 1846. His father was a wealthy Anglo-Irish landlord, his mother an American whose father had fought against Britain in the war of 1812. Parnell was elected Home Rule MP for Co. Meath in 1875. He became President of the Irish National Land League in 1879, and leader of the Parliamentary Party in 1880. He sought land reform for Ireland and believed that once that ambition was realised, then Protestant landlords would support Home Rule, rather than the Union between Britain and Ireland. After the 1885 election, he and his eighty-five MPs held the balance of power at Westminster, but Home Rule measures were defeated in 1886. Three years later Parnell was cited as co-respondent in a divorce case brought about by an Irish MP, whose wife, Katherine O'Shea, had been Parnell's mistress since 1880. He later married her, but by then his popular support had waned, and he lost the leadership of his party. He died in Brighton on 6 October 1891.

The sculptor Richard Barter was born in Macroom, Co. Cork, about 1824. Around the age of twenty he entered the Royal Dublin Society's School. In Dublin he made many friends, including Daniel O'Connell, who took a great interest in his progress. Leaving Ireland, he spent some time in London. He then returned to Ireland and settled in Blarney, Co. Cork. He built himself a studio and worked there for the remainder of his career, with occasional visits to London. He was an artist of considerable talent. His work was always original, and his portrait busts showed the great skill and perception of character so evident in this bronze.

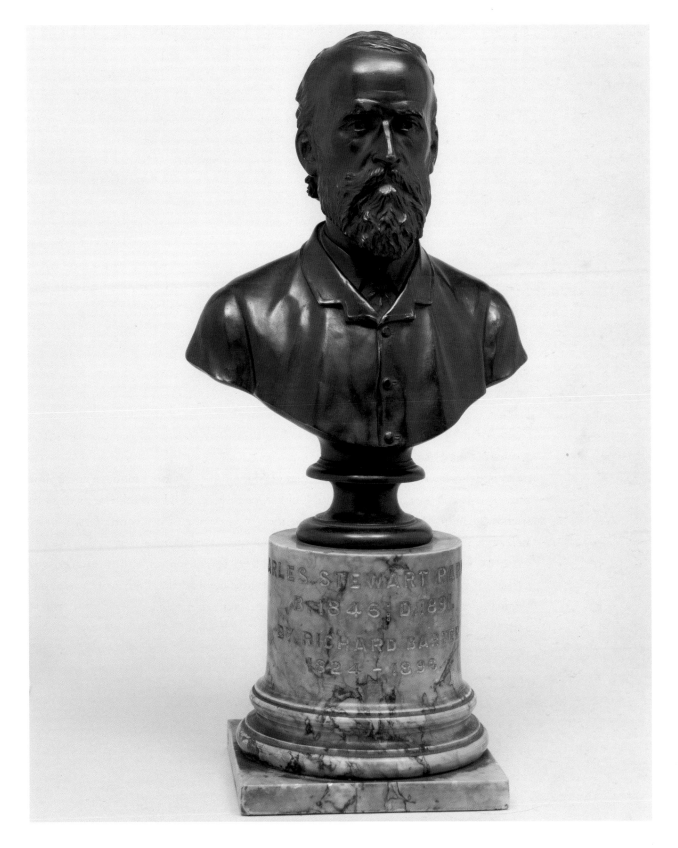

Roderic O'Conor (1860-1940)

LA FERME DE LEZAVEN, FINISTÈRE 1894

Oil on canvas,
72 x 93 cm
NGI NO. 1642

RODERIC O'CONOR is often described as Ireland's first modernist painter due to the fact that his career was bound up with significant European avant-garde developments. He spent most of his career in France, and his legacy of nudes, portraits, still-life and especially landscape painting places him in the forefront of early-twentieth-century Irish art. O'Conor was born in Co. Roscommon of wealthy parents, who came from an old Irish family. He attended the Dublin Metropolitan School of Art and the Royal Hibernian Academy School, *en route* winning many prizes. In 1883 he left Ireland to study at Antwerp, enrolling in the life class of Charles Verlat. In 1886 he moved to Paris to train under Carolus Duran and immediately became aware of contemporary impressionist painting. His move to Brittany enabled him to work with modern artists and his name is automatically linked with the Pont Aven school of painters. O'Conor, who was fortunate in having a private income throughout his life, died in 1940 in France.

The subject of this picture is a seventeenth-century farmhouse which was used by many artists who painted in the small rural Breton village of Pont Aven. O'Conor was one of a large body of painters who were attracted to the striking landscape and people of Brittany. By the end of the 1880s, he had become familiar with the work of Van Gogh, and he became influenced by his style. O'Conor paints in strong, striped brushstrokes, using vibrant colours. He was also friendly with Gauguin and painted with him in Brittany, though he refused the artist's invitation to travel with him to Tahiti. Gauguin had rented the farmhouse illustrated here in 1889, and four years later, in 1893/4, O'Conor used it as his studio. *Farm at Lezaven* is a carefully composed landscape in which the layers of flowers, trees and foliage lead the eye to the sunlit farmhouse in the background. There is a strong use of complementary red, green colours in the foreground, which reflects O'Conor's awareness of colour theory, prefiguring the work of the Fauve painters (1905-8). While he was clearly influenced by Van Gogh and Gauguin, both post-impressionist artists, in their conscious use of unusual or arbitrary colours, O'Conor illustrates in this picture how he pursued his own independent path. The most distinctive feature of this composition is his striped brushstroke technique, which produces a vivid picture surface. This element, combined with his exploration of the intensity of colour, produces a powerful and dramatic modern landscape.

Mildred Anne Butler (1858-1941)

A PRELIMINARY INVESTIGATION 1898

Watercolour on
paper,
65.5 x 97.5 cm
NGI NO. 7952

A Preliminary Investigation reflects Mildred Anne Butler's superb skill in painting birds. In this accomplished watercolour, she portrays a flock of doves gathering around corn, which has spilled from an open sack onto the ground. The birds are carefully observed. Those in the foreground of the composition are captured in varying degrees of profile, and from the rear. Some have their chests puffed up while others crane their necks forward as they investigate their find. Meanwhile, to the rear of this activity, more doves alight, curious to discover what is happening. Their wings are sketchily treated to convey the fluttering motion of descent. The scene is set in the neglected corner of a farmyard, indicated by the empty pails, upturned pots and a broken wooden crate. Bright sunshine filters onto areas of lush green grass and creates dazzling spotlights of white colour on the coats of the doves closest to the sack. Letters survive from 1888 and 1900 from a London taxidermist, from whom Butler bought stuffed specimens of birds, including ducks, woodpigeons, waterhens and rooks, presumably to study their plumage and features. Butler's large depictions of birds depended on stuffed examples and photographs for their accuracy (it would not have been possible to observe the birds closely enough during flight). It is all the more remarkable then, that the artist achieved such spontaneity in her work, which is regarded as one of the greatest qualities in her watercolours. The picture's charm is enhanced by the human characteristics of the birds and by the strong element of narrative. Their small beady eyes are sharp with curiosity as they survey this unexpected feast and one senses that it will be only a matter of moments before they surge forward and fight to devour the corn.

Mildred Anne Butler was born at Kilmurry, near Thomastown, Co. Kilkenny, and spent most of her life living and painting in this tranquil and picturesque area. During the year 1885 she travelled widely in Europe. Later she studied briefly under William Calderon, an animal painter, and also at the painters' colony in Newlyn, Cornwall. She was introduced to *plein-air* painting by the Limerick-born artist Norman Garstin (1847-1926). The artist began exhibiting her work in London and in Ireland in the 1890s and was elected an associate of the Royal Watercolour Society in 1896, becoming a member in 1937. Her subject matter is drawn from the countryside and is evocative of the quiet harmony of her surroundings in Co. Kilkenny.

John Butler Yeats (1839-1922)

PORTRAIT OF WILLIAM BUTLER YEATS 1900

Oil on canvas,
77 x 64 cm
NGI NO. 872

THIS ARRESTING PORTRAIT, painted in 1900, captures the likeness of the distinguished poet and playwright, William Butler Yeats (1865-1939), son of the artist, when he was just thirty-five years old. Though father and son were on good terms, William was often serious, moody and distracted, which made him difficult to deal with. The portrait was painted in London, where William had moved to spend Christmas with his family, having worked with George Moore on the play *Diarmuid and Grania*. This painting, which took three sittings, shows the poet in a striking half-length pose, and it is remarkable for its sensitivity to character and the freshness of its brushwork. William, who is portrayed as a sensitive, scholarly, absent-minded poet, was one of the central figures in the Irish Literary Renaissance, his work inspired by Irish myth and legend. The elder Yeats quite naturally sought a poetic image for his son, and this is skilfully achieved by using a limited palette to draw the pale figure emerging from a dark background. An intensely abstracted image, the poet appears absorbed by the ideas in his mind. A year after its execution, the portrait was purchased by the American collector John Quinn, who befriended the Yeats family. It returned to Ireland in 1926 when it was presented to the National Gallery of Ireland by Mr C. Sullivan in memory of John Quinn.

John Butler Yeats was the father of the most gifted Irish artistic family of the early twentieth century. His son, William, was the Nobel prize-winning poet, his son Jack the foremost contemporary painter, his daughters Susan Mary (Lily) and Elizabeth Corbet (Lolly) were leading members of the arts and crafts movement and founders of the Dun Emer and Cuala Press Industries. After studying law at Trinity College Dublin, John Yeats practised as a barrister until 1867, when he decided to become an artist. He moved to London to study at Heatherley's, and later at the Royal Academy School. Over the years he moved the family frequently between Dublin and London, exhibiting at the Royal Hibernian Academy, where he became a full member in 1892. In 1901 Sarah Purser organised an important joint exhibition with Nathaniel Hone the Younger, which greatly enhanced his career. During the following seven years he painted some of the most distinguished Irish men and women of his day. In 1908 he emigrated to the United States, where he earned an income by painting portraits, writing and lecturing, and he died alone at the age of eighty-three in New York. Portraits such as the one illustrated here, justify the claim that John Butler Yeats was among the most gifted Irish portraitists of his generation. In addition to his much admired painted portraits, he also executed hundreds of masterly portrait sketches in pencil.

Walter Osborne (1859-1903)

THE DOLL'S SCHOOL 1900

Watercolour and
pastel on board,
45.2 x 59.5 cm
NGI NO. 2535

THIS SENSITIVELY OBSERVED scene was painted by Walter Osborne in 1900. It is believed that the little girl is Violet Stockley, a niece of the artist, who also figures in a number of his other compositions. Osborne had studied at the Metropolitan School of Art in Dublin before moving first to Antwerp and then to Brittany. He mixed with many avant-garde artists of the day and was influenced by their treatment of light. He spent time in England during the 1880s, where he painted rural scenes of villages with cottage gardens, just as he had done on the Continent. His return to Dublin in the 1890s was prompted by the need to help support his family. During his short career he established himself as one of Ireland's most gifted artists, creating an oeuvre consisting of portraiture, landscape and genre, some of which reflect his interest in contemporary artistic trends. Most of Osborne's watercolour and chalk drawings are studies, and he exhibited some at at the RHA from 1877 to 1903. He was also a member of the Dublin Sketching Club. This picture was painted three years before the artist's early death from pneumonia.

This watercolour focuses on the intimate world of children at play. The artist is clearly very fond of and comfortable with children. The child plays happily, seemingly unaware of the artist's presence. The young girl kneeling on her bed has lined up her toys. Resting on her knees, she leans forward with one hand pointed as if talking to them. Indeed the little Chinese toy with the black pony-tail seems to be listening intently to her. The artist conveys the essential privacy of this world of make-believe in several ways. The view of the room is deliberately restricted. Only the corner where the iron-cast bed is placed can be seen and a small fraction of the walls, on which are hung small framed pictures. Most important of all, the child is turned away so that only her back and a tiny portion of her face are on view. Light from an unseen window gently illuminates the little private world of her and her companions.

While this late work shows the influence of impressionism in its everyday subject matter and its treatment of light effects, its painting technique is different to that of the impressionists. It demonstrates the artist's talent in combining watercolour and pastel to achieve a particularly spontaneous effect. The brushwork is loose, the light effects are delicately conveyed and the choice of colour is eye-catching, with its mixture of warm creams and browns, offset by strong accents of blue, red and mauve. Children are a regular subject in Osborne's work and he always treated them with sympathy, affection and understanding. The National Gallery of Ireland has several paintings on similar themes.

Paul Henry (1876-1958)

LAUNCHING THE CURRACH 1910-11

Oil on canvas,
41 x 60 cm
NGI NO. 1869

*L*aunching the Currach was painted by Paul Henry in 1910/11, shortly after his arrival on Achill Island, Co. Mayo, at a time when figures predominated in his paintings, whether of islanders digging potatoes, fetching turf, harvesting seaweed or preparing to go fishing. This scene illustrates five fishermen pushing a currach out to sea. This type of boat, still used today, was ideal because of its small size, as it could be carried ashore by the fishermen and it did not need a harbour. The bent posture of the men emphasises the effort of pushing the boat out into the rough Atlantic Ocean. Henry contrasts the slight sailing craft with the turbulent sea, reinforcing the reality of the harsh and uncertain lifestyle of the islanders. Achill was to be the central theme of Henry's artistic life. There he discovered an ideal subject matter in the landscape and sea, which he found had a monumentality that inspired a sense of timelessness. Although these works display a simplicity of composition and execution, demonstrated in precise and assured brushwork that stems from his Parisian training, they also reflect contemporary artists' fascination with seeking simple primitive lifestyles, such as that found in Brittany and the South Sea Islands.

Born in Belfast in 1876, Paul Henry trained initially at the Belfast School of Art before going, in 1898, to Paris, where for a time he studied at the Académie Julian, and then at Whistler's Académie Carmen. In 1900 Henry moved to London, where three years later he married the Scottish artist Grace Mitchell and worked for a decade as an illustrator. He heard about Achill Island from the Belfast writer Robert Lynd, who had been there on his honeymoon. In 1910 the Henrys went on holiday to Achill. In 1912 he abandoned his career as an illustrator in London to move there, making sketches and paintings of Irish people, scenes and landscapes. He remained in Achill until 1919, before returning to Dublin. By the early 1920s Henry's popularity had increased, his technique was assured, and for the rest of his career his style changed little. One of the founders of the Society of Dublin Painters, Henry also exhibited regularly at the Royal Hibernian Academy between 1910 and 1958. Several of his pictures were reproduced as travel posters and became the quintessential image of Ireland. Despite his failing sight, Henry wrote two autobiographies, *An Irish Portrait* (1951) and *Further Reminiscences*, published in 1973.

John Lavery (1856-1941)

THE ARTIST'S STUDIO: LADY HAZEL LAVERY WITH HER DAUGHTER ALICE AND STEP-DAUGHTER EILEEN, 1910-13

Oil on canvas,
344 x 274 cm
NGI NO. 1644

The Artist's Studio depicts John Lavery and his wife Hazel, seen reflected in a mirror as he paints the portrait at his studio in 5 Cromwell Place, London. This group portrait was executed between 1910 and 1913 and could be subtitled *Homage to Las Meninas* by Velázquez, since the composition is based on the painting of the same title in the Prado; the position of the dog, the similarity of the main figures in the foreground of the picture, and the reflection of the artist at work on the portrait in the distant mirror, presents the same type of spatial ambiguity exploited by Velázquez. The Moorish servant, Aida, enters wearing an oriental costume and carrying a salver of fruits. The dog, named Rodney Stone, is included to repeat the dog motif in *Las Meninas*. Above the mantelpiece hangs *Idonia in Morocco — The Equestrian Lady*, the product of his first trip to Morocco, reflecting his interest in travel and orientalism. The queen's portrait, barely visible on the easel, alludes to his significant royal commissions. The foreground group features Hazel Lavery, fashionably dressed in a feathered turban and richly coloured silk and satin Paisley coat. Her daughter Alice is seated in a basket chair, and leaning against the grand piano is Eileen, Lavery's daughter by his first wife. Technically, Lavery was a most accomplished painter, with a refined sense of design and atmosphere, fluid in his handling of paint and excelling in large compositions such as this one.

Lavery was born in Belfast and orphaned at an early age. After studying art in Glasgow and London, he went to Paris in 1881, enrolling in Colarossi's and at the Académie Julian. During 1883 he spent time at the artist's colony at Grez-sur-Loing, where he was influenced by the work of Bastien-Lepage and the Irish painter Frank O'Meara. He returned to Glasgow and in 1890 married Kathleen McDermott, who died shortly after giving birth to their daughter, Eileen. Lavery settled in London, establishing himself as a celebrated portraitist, whose sitters included leading figures of international society. He met Hazel Martyn, daughter of a Chicago industrialist, in 1904, when she was painting in Brittany, and in 1910 they were married. Hazel was thirty years younger and also widowed. A beautiful woman, she became a leading figure in London society and a valuable friend to Ireland through her association with Irish political leaders at the time of the Treaty in 1922. Her political services were rewarded when she was asked to pose for the figure of Cathleen Ní Houlihan, featured on the new Free State currency, which is still used as the watermark on Irish currency notes. Lavery retained his links with Ireland and painted portraits of several ministers of the Irish Free State. During the First World War he served as official artist to the Royal Navy, and in 1918 he was knighted. Lavery died in 1941 at the home of his step-daughter Alice in Co. Kilkenny.

Patrick Tuohy (1894-1930)

SUPPER TIME 1912

Pencil and water-
colour with white
highlights on
paper,
50 x 70 cm
NGI NO. 3306

PAINTED BY TUOHY in 1912, when the artist was only eighteen years old, *Supper Time* represented a promising début for the young artist, winning him the prestigious Taylor Scholarship. An ambitious work, the portrait displays Tuohy's skill at depicting children and adults within a group setting. It is an ambiguous image. Despite the appearance of a family gathering for a light meal, the dominant male figure, portrayed as a middle-aged man, does not appear to have a place setting. The woman in the centre pours milk carefully into a teacup, as though providing for an unexpected guest. There is an Orpenesque influence in the finely drawn figures and setting. While the colours are bright and lively, the clear light brings the features and expressions of each person sharply into focus. The mood is apprehensive and somewhat edgy, compounded by the mysterious face reflected in the window pane.

Patrick Tuohy was born in Dublin, the son of a surgeon. He displayed an early gift for drawing, despite the disability of having been born without a left hand. Supporters of Ireland's struggle for independence, his parents sent him to Patrick Pearse's school, St Enda's in Rathfarnham. There he was encouraged by William Pearse to attend classes at the Metropolitan School of Art. At the School he came under the forceful influence of William Orpen, whose emphasis on life-drawing helped him gain a thorough understanding of the human form. This benefited him later when he became a portrait painter. As a result of winning the Taylor Scholarship in 1912 and 1915, Tuohy was able to go to Madrid. A fervent nationalist, he was involved in the 1916 Easter Rising, fighting in the General Post Office in Dublin. In 1918 he began exhibiting at the Royal Hibernian Academy, teaching for a time at the Metropolitan School of Art. Tuohy was one of the leading painters in the early years of the Irish Free State. A prolific artist, his career encompassed landscapes, religious subjects, ceiling paintings and the most accomplished series of portraits of literary, artistic and political figures of the decade. In 1927 he emigrated to America, where despite success in Columbia, South Carolina and New York, he became depressed, committing suicide at the age of thirty-six. He was buried at Glasnevin Cemetery in Dublin. Tuohy was a quiet, sensitive and introspective artist, whose most famous pupil was Norah McGuinness.

William John Leech (1881-1968)

THE SUNSHADE c.1912

Oil on canvas,
81 x 65 cm
NGI NO. 1246

LEECH'S WORK is divided between paintings executed in France during the early part of his career, and those made later in England. His fascination with the treatment of light in French painting, encouraged him while in Brittany to try creating the effect of sunlight on surfaces. These canvases are flooded with light and colour. *The Sunshade* depicts William John Leech's first wife, Elizabeth, under a green parasol in a sun-drenched garden. Elizabeth modelled for a number of his pictures, most notably *The Convent Garden, Brittany*, also in the National Gallery of Ireland. The painting reveals Leech using a brighter palette, much influenced by post-impressionism. Leech was noted for his precise choice of colour: cadmium yellow was used in the painting of the cardigan, contrasting with the viridian green of the parasol. The artist has used thick brushstrokes skilfully to create the different textures of the cardigan and the umbrella. The strong yellows and greens are repeated in the lilies in the background, with additional colour introduced in the red, purple and lilac of the hat.

William Leech was born in Dublin, the son of wealthy parents. He enrolled at the Metropolitan School of Art in 1899, after which he transferred to the Royal Hibernian Academy Schools in 1900, where Walter Osborne was his teacher. His training was completed at the Académie Julian in Paris. In 1903 he left for Concarneau in Brittany, where, captivated by the Breton environment, he gradually abandoned his academic style, changing to a more fluid, assured manner. In 1910 he was elected a full member of the RHA. Two years later Leech married Saurin Elizabeth Kerlin, but towards the end of the First World War they agreed to a separation. In 1918 Leech was conscripted into the British Army and served six months of the war, ending up in a detention camp in France. On his return to England he became depressed and was unable to paint. In 1919 he met May Botterell, the wife of Percy Botterell, a well-known London lawyer. A relationship developed between the artist and May, about which they were both discreet on account of May's family commitments. She supported him emotionally and financially, and when her husband died in 1952, the couple married. After the First World War, Leech divided his time between England and France, travelling, whenever possible, with May Botterell. Leech's work, initially inspired by Brittany and French painters, gradually became more influenced by English painting. Leech was acclaimed for his portraits, interiors, landscapes and still life, in addition to a remarkable series of self-portraits.

Patrick Michael Joseph Healy (1873-1941)

ST PATRICK LIGHTING THE PASCHAL FIRE ON THE HILL OF SLANE 1914

Ink, pencil and
watercolour on
paper,
27.2 x 28 cm
NGI NO. 18,363

St Patrick Lighting the Paschal Fire on the Hill of Slane, executed by Michael Healy in 1914, was a design for a cinquefoil panel of stained glass for the apex of a two-light window in the Catholic church at Donnybrook, Dublin. A copy was made for the Cranbrook Academy, Bloomfield Hills, Michigan, USA. It depicts St Patrick on the Hill of Slane having lit the Pascal fire, a fire symbolising the mystery of the Resurrection of Christ. The saint is flanked by two angels, while below are the crouching, cowering figure of an Irish warrior chief and a draped bearded man kneeling in supplication. The scene represents a dramatic moment. The choice of place to light this fire was significant as it was near the Hill of Tara, seat of the pagan high kings of Ireland, and so could be seen by King Laoghaire, who had issued a decree against such an action. King Laoghaire (Loegaire), a great and fierce king who died in 458, was a contemporary of St Patrick. The divinely inspired strength of the saint is conveyed by the glowing supernatural light beamed on the figure by the Holy Spirit above. This large figure, which takes up the centre space in the design, creates the impression of a physically and morally powerful man, as do the upraised arms holding the staff aloft and his determined expression.

A Dubliner by birth, Michael Healy enrolled at the Metropolitan School of Art at the relatively late age of twenty-four. Later he attended the Royal Hibernian Academy Schools. He was in Italy in 1899, working mainly in Florence. On the strength of his line drawings, Healy was invited to join the stained-glass studio An Túr Gloine (The Tower of Glass) when it was founded in 1903, and it was there he learned the art of stained glass. This skill consists of adapting small coloured sketches (showing the general effect and colouring of the proposed window) and working to a full-sized cartoon. From this cartoon an outline is made to help the glass-cutter who, having selected suitable pieces of coloured glass, lays them over the full-size outline and cuts them into shape. When all the pieces of glass have been laid, they are painted. The methods of painting, and the means of drawing the lines, modelling flesh and drapery with pigments on the glass, vary according to the technique of individual artists. After painting, the whole is fired in a kiln, an action that is repeated to ensure sufficient saturation of colour. Reassembly, leading and cementing follow, and when the window is finally complete, it is then ready to be erected in its chosen location. Healy proved to be a gifted stained-glass artist, in addition to being a kind and helpful teacher at An Túr Gloine.

William Orpen (1878-1931)

THE HOLY WELL 1916

Tempera on canvas,
234 x 186 cm
NGI NO. 4030

PAINTED BY WILLIAM ORPEN in 1916, *The Holy Well* shows the artist's satirical attitude to Ireland. This is one of a series of three major canvases, the others entitled *Sowing the Seed* and *The Western Wedding*, executed between 1913 and 1916. The picture shows Orpen attempting to express his complex feelings about contemporary Irish life, at the time of the Easter Rising. The scene is based on the old practice when, on 'pattern days', people would gather to pray at a holy site associated with a local saint. It was not customary, however, as shown here, for people to wash themselves at a 'pattern' or to appear nude at a holy site. Keating, who was Orpen's studio assistant at this time, was the model for the rebellious looking figure standing on the holy well. The high cross and ruins suggest an Early Christian monastic setting, where figures in contemporary dress take part in a religious ritual. According to Keating, who provided costumes from the Aran Islands for the picture, the background was composed from drawings carried out at Maam Cross. In the picture Orpen experiments with a different style and technique, using large, flat areas of colour placed in contrast with a frieze of figures in the foreground, while attempting to experiment with a new fresco-like medium.

Born in Dublin in 1878, Orpen was a child prodigy. He won every prestigious award at the Metropolitan School of Art, which he entered at the age of thirteen, followed by the Slade School of Art in London. He divided his time between Dublin and London, where he was a successful society portraitist. Between 1902 and 1914 he provided tuition at the Dublin Metropolitan School of Art, where he revolutionised teaching practice. An extraordinarily versatile and technically brilliant artist, he became a fashionable, highly paid and much-sought-after painter. He was a superb draughtsman, mainly using chalks, ink on paper or watercolour. Orpen served as a war artist during the First World War, producing the series of powerful paintings illustrating the brutality of the conflict, and he was knighted for his service. These pictures did not show action, but the results of war as portrayed in wounded, injured and tortured figures. His personal life was complicated by relationships with beautiful women. By the time he died, aged fifty-three, he had become a sad figure, distant from family and friends. Orpen's contribution to Irish art was as an influential teacher of a generation of Irish artists, including Seán Keating, Margaret Clarke, James Sleator, Patrick Tuohy and Leo Whelan, in addition to his pre-eminence as a painter of portraits, magnificent in tone value and colour.

Oliver Sheppard (1864-1941)

'IN MYSTERY THE SOUL ABIDES' (Matthew Arnold) c.1917

Marble,
62 cm ht.
NGI NO. 8091

THIS MARBLE STATUETTE is immediately striking for its meditative qualities, both in pose and expression. The young girl, with legs crossed to one side, leans her chin on one hand, while the other is placed across her breasts. Gazing into the distance, the eyes are dreamy, yet reflective. She seems totally unaware of the viewer, so deeply absorbed is she in her thoughts. The title of the sculpture, 'In Mystery the Soul Abides', offers a clue as to the subject of her meditation. The line is freely taken from a poem by the English poet Matthew Arnold, entitled *Morality*. In the opening lines the poet reminds the reader:

> *We cannot kindle when we will*
> *The fire which in the heart resides.*
> *The spirit bloweth and is still.*
> *In mystery our soul abides.*

Sheppard's small, quiet, thoughtful figure may be pondering on the enigma of the life-force of the spirit. In keeping with the sentiments of the poem, the artist has attempted to produce a work of exquisite poetic grace. The quality of the carving is superb in every detail, from the delicately wrought strands of hair to the careful delineation of every finger and toe-nail. The naturalistic treatment of the torso is especially striking, the smooth flesh providing a stark contrast to the roughly hewn rock on which she sits.

The sculptor Oliver Sheppard trained at the Dublin Metropolitan School of Art and at the National Art Training School at South Kensington in London. On returning to Dublin at the turn of the century, he worked as an instructor of modelling at the Metropolitan School of Art and later became Professor of Sculpture at the Royal Hibernian Academy. Sheppard's work consists mainly of sculpted portraits and romantic subjects, often of a Celtic flavour. He also designed many of the best-known monuments to Irish patriots. His most famous work, *The Death of Cuchulain*, commemorating all those who died during the Easter Rising of 1916, is located in the General Post Office in O'Connell Street, Dublin.

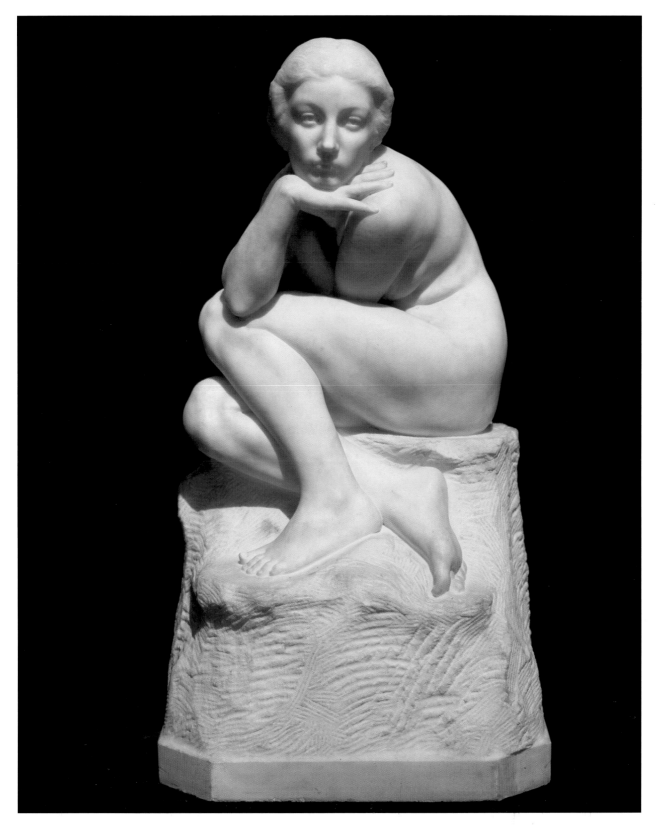

Harry Clarke (1889-1931)

THE SONG OF THE MAD PRINCE 1917

Stained-glass panel,
34.3 x 17.7 cm
(set in a walnut
cabinet made by
James Hicks,
Dublin)
NGI NO. 12,074

The Song of the Mad Prince illustrates a poem by Walter de la Mare of the same title. The scene depicts the distressed prince mourning his dead love. He holds a dagger in one hand and a fan in the other. Behind him are his parents. His father holds a key and at the same time raises his fingers to his lips as if seeking silence; his mother is saying her Rosary. The prince is sumptuously dressed. He wears a white shirt with upturned collar, lined with lace. His cape, a rich blue with touches of red and yellow and edged with white, displays a swirling pattern of undulating, organic shapes. The shoes are elaborately buckled. Technically, this piece of stained glass is among the artist's most impressive creations, with its sensuous colouring and breathtaking variety of detail.

Thomas Bodkin (art connoisseur and a former Director of the National Gallery of Ireland) commissioned this stained-glass panel, which was designed to be placed in a small walnut cabinet with an electric light bulb behind it. It consists of a sheet of blue glass plated against a sheet of ruby glass. Both were intricately worked on with pen and acid to produce a range of four tones in each, plus white. Further acids and stains were applied to create a complete range of colours.

Harry Clarke was one of Ireland's most gifted stained-glass artists. Born in Dublin, he trained first in his father's stained-glass business and from 1910 at the Metropolitan School of Art. In 1914 he won a scholarship which enabled him to study medieval glass in England and in Paris. His reputation was quickly established with a commission to make windows for the Honan Chapel in Cork (1916-17). Clarke took over his father's firm in 1921 and in his short time in charge (he became ill in 1925 and died six years later) he was instrumental in completing over fifty stained-glass commissions for Ireland, Britain and the United States. During his career he produced some exquisite drawings and watercolours. He was also an outstanding graphic artist, illustrating books and executing some fabric designs.

Seán Keating (1889-1977)

AN ALLEGORY C.1922

Oil on canvas,
102 x 130 cm
NGI NO. 1236

An Allegory, painted by Seán Keating around 1922 during the height of the Civil War (1922-23), shows the artist making a profound statement about Ireland in the formative years of the Free State. It is a less than glorious image of war. The scene is set in the grounds of a country house, which has been destroyed due to its association with the past. In the foreground, members of the regular and irregular army dig a grave. The tricolour which covers the coffin may symbolise a sacrifice, or represent the past being buried. Nearby, a priest is engaged in conversation with a businessman, while warily watching the soldiers. The picture reflects the artist's sense of despair at the country in the throes of civil war, with only the mother and child in the centre of the composition expressing any hope for the future. The figure of the man lying exhausted represents the artist. Keating, who had earlier espoused violence as a means to gain independence, glorifying the military struggle in his paintings, was now appalled by the outbreak of fresh conflict. Early in his career Keating was instrumental in developing an image of national identity based on his knowledge of the older Gaelic culture of the Aran Islands. His great achievement was to incorporate this imagery in his art of the 1920s, whilst at the same time in other works recording the State's plans for a modern, industralised society. Keating's mature images helped articulate Ireland's aspiration to be a progressive industrial nation.

Born in Limerick in 1889, Seán Keating attended drawing classes at the local technical school before winning a scholarship in 1911 to the Metropolitan School of Art in Dublin. There he studied painting and drawing until 1914 under William Orpen, the undisputedly great teacher of his generation. Keating became Orpen's favourite pupil, inheriting his reverence for careful drawing and an academic approach to painting. A fervent nationalist, he made his first trip to the Aran Islands in 1914 at the suggestion of Harry Clarke. The islands were a revelation to Keating and he spoke passionately to his students about the unique lifestyle in the west. He began teaching in 1918 at the Metropolitan School of Art, and became its Professor of Painting when it was reconstituted as the National College of Art in 1936, thereby influencing decades of young artists. As a teacher, he was outspoken in his dislike of the modern movement and stood firmly on the side of traditional art.

Mainie Jellett (1897-1944)

DECORATION 1923

Tempera on panel,
89 x 53 cm
NGI NO. 1326

*D*ecoration by Mainie Jellett, along with a similar abstract painting, caused a sensation when it was first exhibited at the Society of Dublin Painters Group Show at 7 St Stephen's Green in 1923. *The Irish Times* reviewer of the exhibition wrote that he could not understand the works: 'They are in squares, cubes, odd shapes and clashing colours. They may, to the man who understands the most up-to-date modern art, mean something; but to me they presented an insoluble puzzle'. The matter was pursued one week later when the newspaper published a photograph of *Decoration* and one of an onion which resembled a bird sitting on a nest. Readers were invited to 'provide a solution' to the puzzle. Another reviewer of the same exhibition talked of the 'sub-human art of Miss Jellett'. This fierce onslaught on the first abstract work to be exhibited in Dublin sparked off a controversy about modern art which was to last for the rest of Jellett's life.

The Dublin-born artist Mainie Jellett revolutionised art in Ireland in the twentieth century. She trained under William Orpen in Dublin and in London under Walter Sickert. In 1921 she joined Evie Hone (who would achieve fame as a stained-glass artist) in Paris, beginning a period of study under André Lhote, who directed his pupils back into classical art and made them study and copy the old masters. Cézanne's way of breaking down his subject matter into shapes (cubes and cylinders) was also instilled into them. Wishing to explore the extreme abstraction of cubism, the two young women next studied under Albert Gleizes, an established cubist artist. Enriched by her contact with modern art and artists in Paris, Jellett's own art is marked by its focus on rhythm and movement, colour and form.

The composition of *Decoration* consists of a number of coloured shapes which are superimposed on one another (Translation and Rotation), creating a sense of depth on the flat surface of the canvas. The relation of the angles of one shape to another encourages the eye of the viewer to explore the work in a circular movement, thus suggesting an internal motion and rhythm. The picture, although abstract, strongly recalls icon painting in the shape of the panel and the use of gold paint. The use of tempera (in which pigment is mixed with egg yolk rather than oil) is yet another link to icon painting. It is a work in which the artist achieves a perfect abstract harmony purely by means of colour and form.

Margaret Clarke (1888-1961)

BATH TIME AT THE CRÈCHE 1925

Oil on canvas,
127 x 101 cm
NGI NO. 4359

Bath Time at the Crèche was painted in the artist's studio in Dublin, inspired by a holiday at Laytown, Co. Meath, with her family. It is a scene that includes her children, while also making references to objects in the Clarke home. The young people illustrated in the top left-hand corner (reading from left to right) are the artist's own children, David, Ann and Michael. In the top right of the canvas a mother, or perhaps a nanny, supervises a group of children. Their identity is unknown. The charming, dark-haired boy in the bottom right-hand corner is Terry Clarke, a nephew of the artist. Intriguingly, the main figure in the painting, Julia O'Brien, who was both the artist's model and nanny to her children, is depicted bathing a small black-skinned child. The reason for this unusual inclusion is that the artist possessed a carved head of a black infant and chose to include it in order to vary the composition. Other items in the picture include a toy pipe being blown by Terry. When filled with water and blown into, the pipe created a musical sound.

Born in Newry, Co. Down, Margaret Crilly first studied art at Newry Technical School and then under William Orpen at the Metropolitan School of Art in Dublin. In 1914 she married a fellow student, Harry Clarke, whose reputation as a stained-glass artist was quickly established. This everyday scene, with its large number of figures in every manner of pose, demonstrates the artist's skill at life-drawing. Clarke was a talented portrait painter and exhibited regularly throughout her career at the Royal Hibernian Academy. The composition is quite unusual for its lack of background detail and makes little concession to a perspectival view of the scene. This creates an interesting tension between the figures, which are three-dimensional but set in an almost flat, two-dimensional space. This picture was painted around 1925 and is signed in the artist's maiden name Crilly, to distinguish her own artistic identity from that of her husband.

Charles Lamb (1893-1964)

LOCH AN MHUILINN 1930s

Oil on board,
40 x 50 cm
NGI NO. 4670

*L*och an Mhuilinn (The Mill Lake), painted in the early 1930s, depicts one of several lakes in Carraroe, a small peninsula off the coast of Connemara, where Charles Lamb settled in the 1920s. The artist often fished on the lake. This view, taken from his boat, depicts the custom of local women who regularly washed and rinsed their clothes in the water, when the lakeside would echo with the sound of storytelling and laughter. The artist was fascinated by the effect on the landscape of the women in their striking costumes and the pattern of the washing. In this picture Lamb shows one woman washing under a heavy, overcast sky which is giving way to a clear, dry day. Having come from an industrial town in Northern Ireland, he was captivated by the ever-changing skies of Connemara, and it is not surprising to find that he was an admirer of John Constable (1776-1837), the English landscapist noted for his studies of sky and cloud formations. Lamb employs a bright, colourful palette to pick out solid details, including cottages, mountains, boats, and the woman washing. His technique changes, however, in the flat treatment of areas such as the sides of the cottage, the lakeside, the stone walls and the reflections on the water. This could have been as a result of the quality of light at that moment, or experimenting with a more abstract technique.

Charles Lamb was born in Portadown, Co. Armagh, and like other Northern painters he began his career as an apprentice house-painter in his father's firm of decorators. Having attended the Belfast School of Art (1913-17), he won a scholarship to the Metropolitan School of Art in Dublin. There, between 1917 and 1922, he was taught by Margaret Clarke, James Sleator, Patrick Tuohy, and Seán Keating, who was the dominant personality at the school, continuing Orpen's legacy of fine drawing. During this time of political unrest and civil war, artists looked towards the west of Ireland for a new sense of national consciousness and identity. Lamb, much influenced by the Irish writer Pádraic Ó Conaire, was encouraged in 1919 to visit Connemara. In 1935 he built a house in Carraroe, from where he hosted an annual exhibition and summer school. In 1938 he was elected a member of the Royal Hibernian Academy. From Carraroe he carried out commissions for University College Galway, and executed illustrations for *Cré na Cille* by Máirtín Ó Cadhain (1932) and *An Tincéara Buí* by Seán Ó Coisdealbha (1962). He showed at major exhibitions in Europe and the United States. While Lamb is remembered for his Irish genre scenes, such as *Dancing at a Northern Crossroads* (1920), he is better known for landscapes and seascapes, representing a lifetime of painting the length and breadth of Connemara.

Jerome Connor (1874-1943)

THE PATRIOT 1932

Bronze,
194 cm ht.
NGI NO. 8353

Tʜɪs ʙʀᴏɴᴢᴇ ʀᴇʟɪᴇꜰ panel was originally intended as part of a memorial dedicated to the men who fought in the Easter Rising of 1916. *The Patriot* depicts a life-size, idealised soldier. The full-length figure with its clenched fist and resolute expression epitomises the qualities of courage and resolve traditionally associated with those involved in war and battle. The open coat, flapping cravat and tousled hair convey a sense of movement to the otherwise impassive figure. The panel was to be inserted into a stone slab, with inscriptions above and below. The text above the figure reads:

> *budh chrodha iad*
> *dtroid, b'uasal iad*
> *mbás, urraidhe poblachta*
> *curaidhe ida-cach*

which translates as 'courageous they were in battle, noble they were in death, founder of a republic of heroes were they all'. Below the bronze there was to be a dedicatory text, '*ar an thiodhlacadh 1932 do/laochraidh seachtmhaine/na cásca*' (dedicated, 1932, to the heroes of Easter Week). Although the bronze is in low relief, with the outlines barely incised in places, the overall effect is of a solid figure in the round. Having initially modelled the work in clay before it was cast into bronze, the artist then worked to achieve a beautiful surface patina, a skill at which Connor was particularly successful.

Jerome Connor was born in Annascaul, Co. Kerry. His father, a stonemason, emigrated to Massachusetts in the United States when Jerome was nine years old. At the age of thirteen he ran away from home, and later in life he claimed to have learnt four trades before the age of twenty-one: signpainter, machinist, stonecutter and sculptor. Connor enjoyed a successful career while in the United States, where he was commissioned to do a number of commemorative monuments, including a statue of Robert Emmet; three bronze copies were cast, one of which was presented to Ireland in 1966 and is located in St Stephen's Green, Dublin. From 1925 on, his career involved living alternately in America and Ireland, with visits to the Continent and England. His most important work in Ireland includes the *Lusitania Peace Memorial*, which is dedicated to the memory of those who died in the sinking of the ship, *Lusitania*, torpedoed off the coast of Ireland in 1915 during the First World War. This important monument is located in Cobh, Co. Cork. The National Gallery of Ireland has two drawings and four blueprints of the design in its Collection.

Harry Kernoff (1900-74)

THE BOER WAR MEMORIAL ARCH 1935

Pencil on card,
23.2 x 27.6 cm
NGI NO. 3194

*T*he Boer War Memorial Arch, drawn in 1935, is a representation of the arch on the corner of St Stephen's Green, facing Dublin's Grafton Street. Known locally as 'Traitor's Gate', the arch is a memorial to soldiers of the Royal Dublin Fusiliers who were killed in the Boer War (1899-1902). This regiment was involved in the first battle of what was a particularly brutal and savage conflict. Led by Kitchener, the British commander-in-chief, who was born in Co. Kerry, many Irishmen joined the British Army to fight, including James Craig (Lord Craigavon) and Erskine Childers. The artist Harry Kernoff had an eye for humorous and anecdotal detail, illustrated in this finely drawn pencil sketch, in which men and women stroll with walking sticks, umbrellas and dogs, and a bicycle merrily winds its way around St Stephen's Green. The drawing forms part of a body of work in which Kernoff evokes a feeling for Dublin between 1922 and 1948, when unemployment and poverty were rife. Executed in his own distinctive style, these works remain a perceptive and often humorous record of Dublin and its working-class citizens.

Kernoff was born in London, the son of a Russian Jewish furniture-maker and a Spanish mother. When he was fourteen his family moved to Dublin, and although apprenticed in his father's business, he attended evening classes at the Metropolitan School of Art under Seán Keating, Patrick Tuohy and Maurice MacGonigal. In 1923 he became the first night-student to win the Taylor Scholarship in painting. This enabled Kernoff to travel to London, Paris and Nova Scotia. He began exhibiting at the Royal Hibernian Academy in 1926, continuing almost every year until 1974. Early in his career Kernoff developed a highly personal style, denoted by a fine linear quality more associated with woodblock printing, of which he was an exceptionally accomplished practitioner. His involvement with literary and theatrical figures resulted in an impressive series of portraits, painted in a direct, realistic style, documenting the leading Irish performers of the mid twentieth century. While he illustrated the countryside, especially around Kerry and Connemara, Kernoff essentially chronicled Dublin, leaving a unique record of Ireland's capital city and its citizens. Also a graphic artist, he produced book illustrations and designs for theatre and costumes. He died on Christmas Day in 1974.

Seán O'Sullivan (1906-64)

JAMES JOYCE 1935

Red chalk and
charcoal with white
highlights on grey
paper,
54.5 x 38 cm
NGI NO. 3037

JAMES JOYCE (1882-1941), novelist, poet and dramatist, was born in Dublin. He studied languages at University College Dublin, tried to study medicine in Paris and even considered making a career as a singer before deciding to devote himself to writing. His first novel, *Portrait of the Artist as a Young Man*, was begun while he was still a student and is largely autobiographical. In 1904 he left Ireland to live on the Continent, moving between France, Italy and Switzerland. His novel *Dubliners*, published in 1914, is a series of sharply observed vignettes of Dublin life. In 1922 his masterpiece and most controversial novel, *Ulysses*, was published. This book proved to be the turning point for modern literature. *Ulysses* records in minute detail one day in the life of a single character, Leopold Bloom. Because of the frank nature of the text, the book was banned in the United States and Britain for some years until 1936, when it became available in both countries. Joyce worked for seventeen years on what he considered to be his major work, *Finnegans Wake*, a multi-layered, multi-lingual, epic novel which was published in 1939.

This portrait of the writer is by Seán O'Sullivan, one of Ireland's most gifted draughtsmen. The drawing, in chalk and charcoal on grey paper, was done in 1935 during one of his many visits to Paris. O'Sullivan had trained at the Dublin Metropolitan School of Art, in London and then in Paris. A superb technician and draughtsman, his reputation rests largely on his small portrait drawings in pencil, chalk or pastel, which provide a Who's Who of Irish society from the late 1920s to the early 1960s. O'Sullivan argued that each sitter should be portrayed 'as dispassionately as a piece of still life'. In this head-and-shoulders portrait, Joyce is depicted in three-quarter profile. Although lightly sketched, the use of white highlights modelling the head help to convey the impression of a figure in the round, rather in the manner of sculpted portraits. The artist creates an accurate, objective likeness of his sitter, whom he was acquainted with, and there is no attempt to improve on Joyce's sharp, bird-like features. A sense of the keen intelligence of the writer is conveyed in the meditative pose and expression.

Jack P. Hanlon (1913-68)

FIERY LEAVES, 1935/8

Watercolour on
paper,
66.5 x 49 cm
NGI NO. 6888

THE WATERCOLOUR *Fiery Leaves* by Father Jack Hanlon was bequeathed by the artist to the National Gallery of Ireland. Hanlon's early style can be seen in a series of studies, dating to between 1935 and 1938, displaying fine drawing and meticulous attention to detail. This contrasts with his later style from the 1940s onwards, when he adopted a more fluid, freer approach. The watercolour shows how French influences informed much of Hanlon's painting, particularly Lhote's cubist approach, but also fauvist ideas of pure, bright colour and decorative patterns. Hanlon shared the Fauve group's love of Mediterranean colour and this watercolour reflects a shared affinity with a brighter palette. The vase, painted with a superb economy of line, provides a secure base for the riot of colour, pattern and shape which unfolds over the picture, emphasised by the unpainted areas of paper. Although he painted in oils, his most accomplished work is in watercolour.

While known as a competent painter of figure compositions and religious subjects, the Rev. Jack P. Hanlon is acclaimed for his much-sought-after light, airy, delicate-coloured watercolours of flowers. This Dublin-born artist, who was educated at Belvedere College, Clonliffe College and Maynooth College, was ordained a priest in 1939. In London he attended the Ablett Studios, passing the exam of the Royal Drawing Society. During the late 1930s he trained with Mainie Jellett in Dublin, who was a major influence, introducing him to cubism. Following this, when time permitted, Hanlon studied under André Lhote in Paris, where he was also advised by Henri Matisse. During wartime, this priest-painter designed a series of cards for publication. The Royal Hibernian Academy's rejection of progressive painting in 1942 resulted in the setting up of the Irish Exhibition of Living Art in 1943, of which Hanlon was a founder member, remaining on their committee until 1968. The IELA provided a forum for many artists working in Ireland in new modern styles outside of the academic realist tradition. For a number of years the Department of Education allowed the RHA and IELA to hold their exhibitions in the premises of the National College of Art. Hanlon won many awards and his work was included at shows in London, Paris, Brussels, New York, South America and Ireland. He produced a remarkable body of work during his lifetime which, on his death in 1968, was bequeathed to friends and institutions, including the National Gallery of Ireland.

Leo Whelan (1892-1956)

SELF-PORTRAIT c.1940

Oil on canvas,
107 x 91.5 cm
NGI NO. 4599

THIS ARRESTING self-portrait of Leo Whelan was reputedly painted about 1940 in the artist's studio at 7 Lower Baggot Street in Dublin. It is informal and very different in style to his official portraiture. Presented wearing a matador's coat with a dashing bow-tie and hat, the artist's figure is counterbalanced by a decorative vase in the background. The portrait is Orpenesque in composition, with its direct approach to the sitter, the head superbly executed, and the artist's face frankly observed, revealing a sharp, astute eye that proved indispensable during portrait commissions. There is a sense of wry amusement about this portrait, as though Whelan, having made the decision to reproduce his own image, has intentionally depicted the head and shoulders in a fine and detailed manner, leaving the area of the hands holding the palette and brushes, largely unfinished. The fluid painting of this area gives the impression that it is a preparatory study and creates a remarkably modern feel to the portrait.

The Dublin-born artist Leo Whelan enrolled at the Metropolitan School of Art in 1908, where he studied principally under William Orpen, the most influential teacher of his generation. His competent portrait style owed much to Orpen in its reliance on strong composition and a realistic approach to the sitter. In 1916 he won the Taylor Prize for *The Doctor's Visit* (National Gallery of Ireland), a picture that records an actual event in which his cousin, mother and sister participated. Quiet, Dutch-influenced interior scenes became a common feature of Whelan's genre pictures. Between 1911 and 1956 he contributed to each Royal Hibernian Academy exhibition and was made an academician in 1924. During the 1930s and 40s he was acclaimed for his distinctive portraits of Irish twentieth-century public figures and his accomplished genre painting. Whelan's approach was direct, realistic and unpretentious, favouring a restricted palette and dark tones, differing from the more flamboyant style of some of his contemporaries. He contributed to the *Exposition d'Art Irlandais* in Paris in 1922, was awarded a medal at the 1926 Tailteann Games, and in 1930 he helped organise an exhibition of Irish art at the Musées des Beaux Arts in Brussels. Whelan died of leukaemia in 1956.

Susan Mary (Lily) Yeats (1866-1948)

CORNFIELD WITH POPPIES 1941

Silk thread
embroidered on
blue poplin,
25.5 x 28 cms
NGI YMUS Y9

Cornfield with Poppies has been created in embroidery rather than in the more traditional art media. Silk threads of different shades have been employed on a background fabric of poplin. A rural scene is depicted in which the distant hill is framed by tall foxgloves and meadowsweet. Daisies and poppies crowd the verge near the foreground fence and beyond a field of ripe corn is plainly visible. The three-dimensional nature of the scene has been enhanced by varying thicknesses of thread, employing different types of stitches, and grading the colour from strong to pale in the background. French knot-and-chain stitches help to give the impression of the actual texture of the flowers. The sense of distance in the mountain is achieved by a subtle gradation of shades of thread and by allowing the deep blue background to show through between the stitches. The picture was worked in 1941 for a cousin of the artist, David Meredith, who was then aged sixteen.

Susan Mary (Lily) Yeats, sister of William Butler Yeats and Jack B. Yeats, was born in Sligo. When the family settled in London in 1887, she was apprenticed to May Morris, who ran an embroidery workshop. May was a daughter of William Morris, a pivotal figure in the arts and crafts movement in England during the second half of the nineteenth century. Lily stayed with the Morris firm for six years. From 1899 she exhibited embroidery with the newly established Arts and Crafts Society of Ireland. When, in 1902, Evelyn Gleeson founded an arts and crafts co-operative for women, on the lines of the Morris workshop, Lily and her sister Elizabeth Corbet (Lolly) joined her. The enterprise, known as the Dun Emer Guild, was situated at Dundrum in Dublin. The name derived from Emer, the wife of the ancient Celtic hero Cuchulain, who was renowned for her needlework. The intention of the Guild was to mirror the quality of early Celtic art in modern forms using only Irish materials. The range of the manufactured goods included embroidered items, furniture, carpets, jewellery and other related craft objects. A printing press was also launched, run by Lolly Yeats. However, owing to disagreements with Evelyn Gleeson, the founder, the Yeats sisters set up the Cuala Industries and Press themselves in 1908. During thirty years of printing, sixty books were produced, as well as hand-coloured prints and Christmas cards. The Yeats sisters played an important role in Irish cultural life through the establishment of their businesses.

Mary Swanzy (1882-1978)

CLOWN BY CANDLELIGHT 1942/3

Oil on panel,
14 x 9 cm
NGI NO. 1415

Mary swanzy was a champion of modernism in Irish art. One of a number of gifted women artists, such as Grace Henry, Mainie Jellett and Evie Hone, Swanzy grew up in Ireland at the turn of the century. Born in Dublin, the daughter of an ophthalmic surgeon, she received her education in Dublin, followed by France and then Germany. During 1900 she studied in May Manning's studio, where John Butler Yeats was the visiting tutor. She also studied sculpture under John Hughes at the Metropolitan School of Art. Fortunate enough to have a private income, she was able to devote her life to painting. In 1905/6 she visited Paris, studying under Delacluse and in the studios of de la Granadara, Colarossi and La Grande Chaumière. During those early years in Paris she was influenced by post-impressionism and cubism, which later informed her work. On her return to Dublin, she had a successful portrait practice. However, after the death of her parents, she began to travel, acquiring material for her work *en route*. In 1919/20 she went to Yugoslavia and Czechoslovakia, followed in 1923/4 by travelling to Hawaii and Samoa, exhibiting her work later in Honolulu, Hawaii and California. She paid brief visits to Dublin and Paris before moving to Blackheath in London, where she lived for the rest of her life. While Swanzy is well known for her oils, she also executed fine chalk drawings. She continued to paint until she died at the age of ninety-six years.

The following words are inscribed on the reverse of this picture: 'Clown by Candlelight was painted by me in the preceding year 1942/3, Mary Swanzy'. During the mid-1930s Swanzy's style changed from a lyrical cubism to naturalistic landscapes and figure studies. This period was denoted by private symbolic paintings. Between 1939 and 1945 her works became full of foreboding and disaster. Her house in London was bombed, so she moved to Dublin, where this picture was painted. The Second World War moved her deeply, with consequent profound effects on her art. She filled canvases with despairing, tortured figures representing not the front-line images of battle but the effect of war on the psyche. The subject of the clown is familiar, having been already treated by Watteau, Rouault and Picasso, thus lending a 'French' feel to the picture. The clown, a sad and lonely figure, has been depicted gazing reflectively at the candle as though trying to foresee the future. The flickering candle and omnipresent shadows represent the troubled, uneasy mid-war period. The clown's dominant figure and presence in the picture has been used by the artist to convey her own deep feelings of hope and uncertainty for the future. Swanzy, an original and unconventional figure, while European by training, was a truly international artist.

Gerard Dillon (1916-71)

THE LITTLE GREEN FIELDS 1945

Oil on canvas,
40.5 x 89 cm
NGI NO. 4520

AN IMPORTANT EVENT for Gerard Dillon was the discovery of Connemara in 1939 with his friend George Campbell, and it was there, in 1945, that he painted *The Little Green Fields*. Like many North of Ireland artists, such as Paul Henry and Charles Lamb, he found in Connemara a landscape and lifestyle that retained unbroken continuity with its Gaelic past. In this part of Ireland, largely removed from political turmoil, Dillon observed people living in close communities, leading simple lifestyles, and preserving customs and traditions from generation to generation. During his time there he visited the Aran Islands and lived for a while on the island of Inishlackan, beyond Roundstone. *The Little Green Fields* features quintessential west of Ireland imagery: drystone walls, fields with cattle and horses, high crosses in graveyards, whitewashed cottages with pigs, ruined castles and megalithic tombs. Inhabiting this rural landscape are farmers sowing seed-potatoes and feeding hens. In the foreground, a white monastic figure carved in stone may allude to an earlier time in history, when Ireland was described as an island of 'saints and scholars'. Dillon's view of the landscape was conveyed in an intentionally naïve, primitive manner, which was largely the result of being a self-taught artist. This primitive style enabled Dillon's stated ambition of painting with an innocent, child-like vision to be successfully achieved.

Gerard Dillon was born in the Falls Road, Belfast. He left school at fourteen to become an apprentice painter and decorator. Following a short stint at the Belfast School of Art, he went to London in 1934, which he loved for its anonymity and where he freed himself from the claustrophobic atmosphere of Belfast. During this time he made extended visits to Connemara, Dublin and Belfast. In 1941 he moved to Dublin, joining the White Stag Group, and the following year Mainie Jellett launched his first one-man show. From 1943 he began exhibiting regularly at the Royal Hibernian Academy, and from 1944 with the Irish Exhibition of Living Art. After the war Dillon returned to England, where between 1945 and 1968 he taught at schools in West London. During the 1950s Spanish themes appear in his work as a result of a visit to Spain. His late work was concerned with the subject of death (three of his brothers died of heart disease) and with the role of the artist as a clown or pierrot in society. Apart from painting, he produced etchings, stage sets and designs for murals and tapestries. Dillon spent his remaining years in Dublin, where he died. He is buried in Belfast.

Evie Hone (1894-1955)

THE COCK c.1947

Stained-glass panel,
55.5 x 33 cm
NGI NO. 12066

*T*he Cock, also known as 'The Cock and Pot' and 'The Betrayal', is a stunning stained-glass panel in which shape, colour and pattern are skilfully deployed, revealing Hone's technical brilliance and instinctive understanding of this medium. While the work is denoted by the bold reduction of subject and narrative to their most essential, it is distinguished by the bright, jewel-like quality of the precisely selected stained glass. Based on an episode from the Passion, the panel illustrates the moment when Peter, having denied to a servant that he was a disciple of Jesus, hears the cock crow, exactly as it had been foretold by Christ. The figure of Peter and the servant can be discerned in a small light at the top right corner of the panel. The cock dominates the panel, head upright, crowing loudly, his sharply defined outline enclosing different shapes, colours, painted and textured glass, bound by lead, with cement rubbed between the pieces to make the panel watertight. A deeply private and spiritual person, Hone converted to Catholicism in 1937, which affirmed her determination to revitalise Irish religious art.

Evie Sydney Hone was born into a Dublin banking family with a proud tradition and background of artists. Stricken with polio at the age of eleven, Hone was thereafter lame, which made her even more determined to become an artist. In London she studied at the Byam Shaw Art School, moving in wartime to the Central School of Art, where she was taught by Bernard Meninsky, who encouraged her to go to Paris. It was at Westminster Art School, where she trained under Walter Sickert, that she met Mainie Jellett (1897-1944), her lifelong friend. Hone was in Paris by 1920, followed by Jellett in 1921, where the two studied, first with André Lhote, then Albert Gleizes, an artist who developed a form of cubist abstract painting. In the 1930s, after working as a painter for several years, she turned to stained glass. While Hone's first panels were executed under Wilhelmina Geddes in London, in 1933 she joined the stained-glass studio An Túr Gloine (The Tower of Glass), where she worked until Sarah Purser's death in 1943. She opened her own studio in 1944 at Marley Grange, Rathfarnham, where she established herself as a leading artist of her generation in this medium, obtaining major commissions in Ireland and abroad. Hone's stained glass was inspired by several sources: the discipline of cubist training, the influence of early Italian painters and the French religious painter Rouault, an appreciation of the windows in French cathedrals, and her interpretation of medieval Irish figurative carving. From this emerged an artist who produced some of Europe's finest stained glass in the early twentieth century, her best-known commission being the great window at Eton College Chapel (1949-52). Hone died in Dublin in 1955.

Jack B. Yeats (1871-1957)

THE SINGING HORSEMAN 1949

Oil on canvas,
61 x 91.5 cm
NGI NO. 4524

The Singing Horseman is one of Jack B. Yeats' most joyous, exultant works, expressing an extraordinary degree of freedom and rapport with the environment. Here is a splendid fusion of sea, sky, fields, mountains and islands in complete harmony with human and animal life. All of the individual components are united in one sublime rhythm. The young man, portrayed like a gypsy, is mounted on a superb yellow horse. He sings his heart out in complete accord with the horse, who echoes his mood of lyrical abandonment. By the time it was painted in 1949, the artist had lived through two World Wars, the Easter Rising and the establishment of the Irish Free State. After the death of his wife Cottie in 1947, he sank into deep loneliness, and to ease his pain he completed a number of emotive pictures such as this one. As the artist grew older his ideas became visionary, his imagination fired more by memories of his boyhood in Sligo and the mythological world of Tír na nÓg, land of peace and eternal youth, than by contemporary life. In this picture he has used colour and vivid brushwork to express the deepest feelings of hope and freedom, aroused by his emotions.

Jack Butler Yeats was born in London in 1871, son of John Butler Yeats, the portrait painter, brother of the poet William, while his sisters Lily and Lolly were founders of the Dun Emer and Cuala Press Industries. His formative years (1879-86) were spent with his Pollexfen grandparents in Sligo. Back in London by 1887, he attended art school at South Kensington, and by 1888 he had begun establishing himself as an illustrator for magazines and journals. In 1897 he moved to Devon with his wife Mary Cottenham White (Cottie) and began painting in watercolour and then in oils. During 1905 he toured the poorest parts of the west of Ireland, providing illustrations for J. M. Synge's articles for the *Manchester Guardian*. By 1910, having settled in Ireland, he was consistently painting in oils, loving the fluid texture of the medium. In 1916 he was made a full member of the Royal Hibernian Academy. His style went from an early descriptive, narrative manner, in which the works are carefully composed and painted in muted colours, to work that is more fluid, with less defined outlines and a greater use of unmixed colour. It was his late great expressive works, executed through the use of primary colour and vivid brushwork, that gained him an international reputation. Not alone a painter, but a graphic artist, novelist and play-wright, Jack B. Yeats became the most prominent figure in Irish art in the twentieth century.

Hilda van Stockum (b.1908)

PORTRAIT OF EVIE HONE IN HER STUDIO 1952

Oil on canvas,
51 x 41 cm
NGI NO. 4205

Evie Hone in her Studio, painted in 1952, represents Hilda van Stockum's personal tribute to her mentor. Evie Hone (1894-1955) was one of the founders of the Modern Movement in Ireland, and a member of the renowned Hone family, which provided Ireland with gifted artists over the centuries. Hone's early cubist-inspired abstract paintings gave way in 1933 to stained-glass work, which proved to be her true medium. While Van Stockum was living in Dublin, she befriended Hone and had a chance to observe the artist working in her studio at Marley Grange in Rathfarnham. Illustrated in profile, the artist is shown seated on a high wooden chair, totally absorbed in her work, with her miniature poodle, 'Silver', seated beside her. In the background, a piece of her stained glass is suspended in front of the window, and beside it is a crucifix. The studio is replete with pots of paint, brushes, packing cases, paintings on stretchers in wooden racks and other bric-à-brac. The navy coat folded over the chair was owned by Tommy Kinsella, the glazier who assembled all Hone's windows. Emmie, her maid, in addition to looking after the artist (Hone suffered from polio), also helped with the waxworks. There are echoes here of the Dutch old masters, particularly Vermeer, who greatly influenced Van Stockum.

Although Van Stockum was born in Rotterdam in 1908 of a Dutch father and half-Irish mother, she received her training at the Metropolitan School of Art in Dublin, where, between 1924 and 1927, she was taught by Seán Keating and Patrick Tuohy. From 1927 to 1931 she studied at the Rijks Academie in Amsterdam under Roland Holst and Hendrick Wolter. Van Stockum was later able to direct Hone, in 1933, towards Holst, a noted stained-glass artist, who confirmed that stained glass was her calling. On her return to Dublin she met Ervin Ross Marlin, an American, who later became her husband. During 1931, when they moved to America, Van Stockum attended the Corcoran School of Art in Washington DC. Some years later, in 1955, she worked in the studio of André Lhote in Paris. While Van Stockum is mainly known as a still-life painter of great technical ability, she is an extremely able portraitist and a well-respected writer and illustrator of children's books. In 1983 she was elected an honorary member of the Royal Hibernian Academy, and in 1991 was the subject of a major retrospective at the Academy. The artist, now in her nineties, lives and works in England, surrounded by her children and grandchildren, several of whom are artists.

Patrick Hennessy (1915-80)

THE ORACLE 1960s

Oil on canvas,
109 x 140 cm
NGI NO. 4491

The Oracle by Patrick Hennessy is a somewhat mysterious painting, in which are depicted two incomplete figures, recalling sculpted figures from ancient Greece. The bent figure on the right with hand on head seems to be in silent communication or prayer, while the figure to his left stands solidly upright, staring unseeingly into space. The title suggests that the subject matter concerns the practice in Greece of consulting the Oracle at Apollo's shrine of Delphi to seek a blessing on an enterprise about to be undertaken. Apollo's priestesses would go into a trance before giving their predictions from the gods. The standing figure recalls a famous Greek statue called the *Delphic Charioteer*, representing the winner of the race at the Pythian Games in 472 BC. The figure to the right of the picture is thought to be imaginary but reminiscent of figure types from temple pediments. There is no written evidence that the charioteer ever consulted with the Oracle to ask whether he would or would not win the race but perhaps artistic licence is being used here to suggest that a member of the chariot team is requesting the outcome of the race in advance.

Patrick Hennessy was a painter of still life, landscape and *trompe-l'oeil* (illusionist painting planned to deceive the eye). Born in Cork, he trained at the Dundee College of Art and a travelling scholarship enabled him to study in Paris and Rome. He returned to Ireland at the outbreak of the Second World War, where his technical finesse immediately attracted attention. He liked to work in a consistent, low-key, monochromatic palette. His pictures are unsettling in that while they are realistically depicted, there are elements that leave the viewer uneasy. Flesh tones are depicted in such a way as to suggest the certainty of ultimate decay, as are mouldering statuary and ruined façades. His melancholic landscape creates a world in which nature is barren.

The Oracle is a disturbing picture for several reasons. The depiction of the marble, with its broken pieces and pocked surfaces, reminds us of the power of time over everything, even hard materials like stone. The unincised eyes of both figures, with their hypnotically chilling gaze, recall robot rather than human figures. The bare canvas lacks any background detail and provides no clue as to the intention of the artist. It is a haunting, unsettling, but very striking picture.

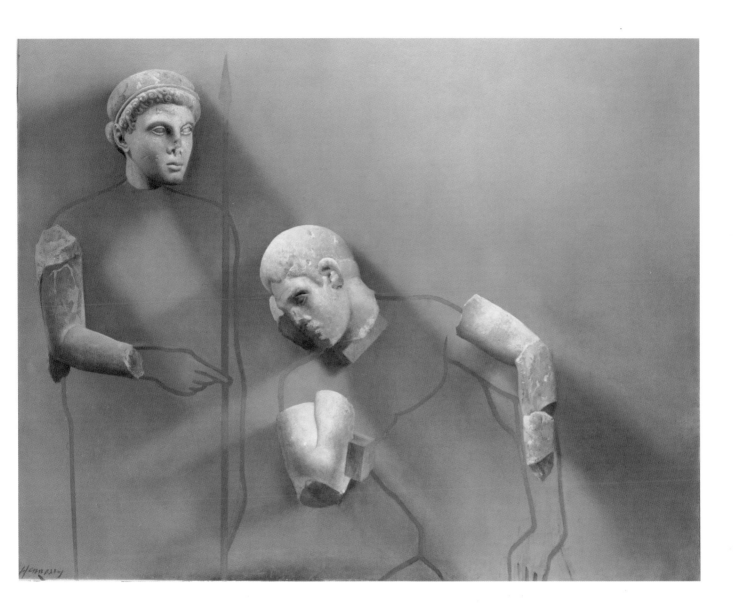

Maurice MacGonigal (1900-79)

EARLY MORNING, CONNEMARA, c.1965

Oil on board,
55 x 75.5 cm
NGI NO. 4461

*E*arly Morning, Connemara is a late work by Maurice MacGonigal, who once said that despite living in Dublin, the west of Ireland, through its people and landscape, provided him with a major source of inspiration throughout his life. In common with other artists who turned to the west of Ireland, such as Paul Henry, Harry Clarke, Seán Keating, Charles Lamb and Gerard Dillon, MacGonigal discovered there an unspoiled landscape and a simple lifestyle, which provided material from which to forge a new national identity. While his early figurative paintings of Connemara followed the nationalistic, academic tradition of Seán Keating, in his later lyrical western landscapes such as *Early Morning Connemara*, painted about 1965, his style became more fluid and spontaneous, with a notably brighter palette. It is clear that while the scene depicts a man crossing a field with a dog and some sheep, the artist is obviously more interested in the great rugged, panoramic landscape of Connemara, with Mannin Bay in the distance. The smoothly executed sky sets the mood, in contrast with the landscape, freely painted in a rapid, energetic manner, creating the effect of a breathtaking scene. MacGonigal will be remembered for his well-observed west-of-Ireland landscapes, which have a distinctive place in the development of landscape painting this century. The artist is buried at Gorteen Cemetery, Roundstone, Co. Galway.

Maurice MacGonigal, a Dublin-born artist, was the son of a Sligo painter and decorator. His training as an apprentice in the stained-glass studios of his uncle, Joshua Clarke, was interrupted by his involvement in the War of Independence (1919-21), as a result of which, in 1920, he was arrested and interned, being released in 1922. His years as a soldier helped him to form his artistic vision. After the Treaty he resumed his training with his cousin Harry Clarke, with whom he produced a number of stained-glass designs. MacGonigal obtained a scholarship enabling him to study full time at the Metropolitan School of Art between 1923 and 1926, where Keating, Sleator and Tuohy were teachers. A trip to Holland in 1927 to see the Dutch masters was influential, particularly the work of Van Gogh. In 1924 he began exhibiting at the Royal Hibernian Academy, becoming a full member in 1933, Keeper in 1950 and President of the Academy in 1962-78 (also their Professor of Painting). For most of his life (1937-69) he taught painting at the National College of Art and Design, where he succeeded Keating as Professor of Painting. He was also a designer of stage sets, posters and book illustrations. His death in 1979 marked the end of a generation of artists, much influenced by Orpen, who were significant in forging a sense of national identity for independent Ireland.

Anne Yeats (b.1919)

WOMEN AND WASHING, SICILY 1965

Oil on canvas,
61 x 91.5 cm
NGI NO. 4613

THIS STRIKING picture was painted by the artist after a visit to Sicily in 1965. Anne Yeats spent six weeks touring the countryside, and as she explored she sketched what interested her. As a result, several paintings of the region were executed, almost all of them brightly coloured. *Women and Washing, Sicily*, however, is notable for its absence of colour. Using a sombre palette relieved by small patches of white and grey, she depicts three women resting from their domestic chores. The woman seated on the right holds a bowl in her hands. It is filled with an unidentified green substance, perhaps some vegetables, needing preparation for a family meal. Her moment of rest, it is implied, will be short-lived. Meanwhile her companions, in almost identical poses, heads slightly drooping, hands placed on their knees, also take advantage of the brief lull from their busy lives. They sit still, lost in thought, as if in a private world of their own, where the daily grind can temporarily be forgotten. The artist forgoes detail in favour of simple, abstracted forms. There is a striking contrast between the cool, shadowy areas in which the three women take shelter and the hot Italian light of the open street. Here the white linen clothes, washed earlier by them, are bleached dry in the glaring heat of the sun. They create a pretty pattern of shapes and break up the composition into three distinct sections of dark, light and dark.

Anne Yeats, daughter of the poet William Butler Yeats, was born in Dublin and at the age of thirteen went to study at the Royal Hibernian Academy Schools. After a visit to Spain, she joined the Abbey Theatre in Dublin as an assistant stage designer. After a period at the Paul Collin School of Theatre Design in Paris, she returned to the Abbey as chief designer, sometimes preparing sets for the plays of her father and uncle (Jack B. Yeats). During the 1940s she became a painter. She had a special interest in techniques involving ink or watercolour and wax. Later she turned to oil and to figure studies. Many of these centred on women and the theme of loneliness and isolation. Her stance, however, was not simply that of the objective observer. She felt a personal empathy with them, declaring that they 'are probably me'. In these paintings she draws attention to the gulf that separates people, regardless of their physical proximity. This Sicilian scene explores that same theme. The women, although placed close together, are nevertheless separated by space and by their individual thoughts.

Edward McGuire (1932-86)

PORTRAIT OF SEAMUS HEANEY 1974

Tempera on panel,
31 x 23 cm
NGI NO. 4112

THIS PORTRAIT depicts the Nobel laureate, Seamus Heaney, as a young man in 1974. In keeping with the fashion of the period, his glossy black hair falls around his forehead and ears. He wears a dark grey, Aran-knit sweater. In spite of its small size, the portrait exercises a compelling presence. The tight, close-up view ensures that nothing distracts from the strongly lit, craggy features and relentlessly piercing gaze. No background detail intrudes. The thick strands of hair act as a framing device for the face. The individually worked stitches of the sweater, so precisely painted, draw the eye upward again and again to the powerfully observed head. The artist, working in a highly stylised, photo-realist way, successfully conveys the physical and intellectual presence of his sitter. Heaney was born in 1939 in Co. Derry and obtained a degree from Queen's University, Belfast. In 1972 he moved south, first settling in Ashford, Co. Wicklow. That sojourn produced *Wintering Out* (1972) and *North* (1976). In the course of the next two decades he held teaching posts in Dublin, Belfast, and then at the University of California at Berkeley. He was Professor of Poetry at Oxford (1989-94), followed by Boylston Professor of Rhetoric at Harvard. He has been accorded most of the literary honours to be won in Ireland and internationally. In 1995 he was awarded the most prestigious international award, the Nobel Prize for Literature.

Edward McGuire was a leading portraitist in a 'neo-Byzantine' mode: full-frontal treatments of static, stylised subjects. Born in Dublin, he showed an early interest in drawing and painting. He attended the Academy of Fine Art in Rome in 1952/3 and then went on to study at the Slade School of Fine Art in London. As well as painting portraits the artist was a fine painter of still life. McGuire became closely involved with artists and writers in the Dublin scene. A meticulous craftsman, he arranged and graded his colours and tones with scientific accuracy. He often destroyed work that did not satisfy him. Much of his spare time was spent reading poetry and literature. Not surprisingly, many of his portraits were of literary figures, including Eilis Dillon, Seán Ó Faoláin and Anthony Cronin. A larger version of this portrait is in the Ulster Museum, Belfast.

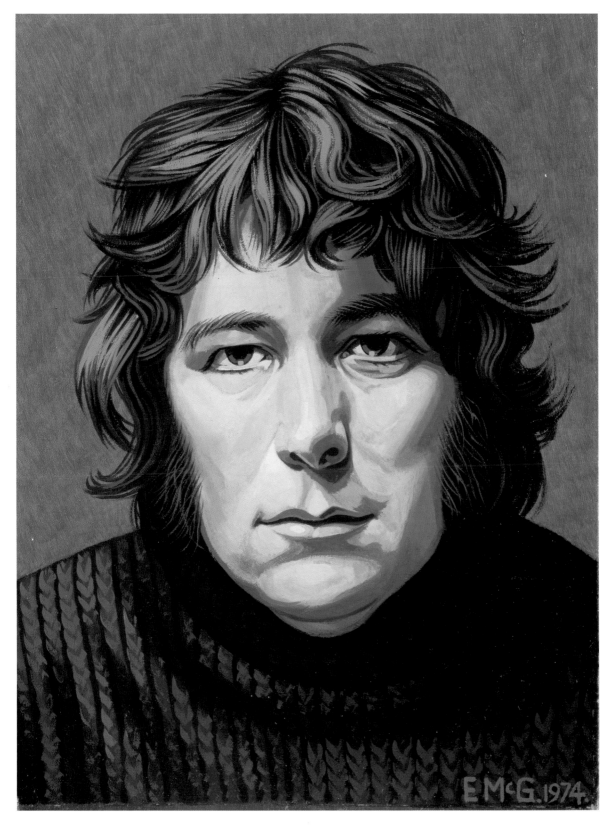

Robert Ballagh (b.1943)

PORTRAIT OF NOEL BROWNE (1925-97) 1985

Oil on canvas,
183 x 137 cm
(six panels of
equal size making
a cruciform shape)
NGI NO. 4573

THIS *Portrait of Noel Browne* is one of Robert Ballagh's personal favourites. The artist chose to paint Dr Browne, a man of integrity and a patriot, because he felt he had contributed to the quality of Irish life, though he made no financial gain. Browne was an inspired and courageous Minister for Health, who fought for the eradication of TB. The painting was not intended to be cruciform but rectangular; however, as it evolved, the artist changed the shape, and as a result the picture is frequently interpreted as an allusion to martyrdom and conflict with the Church. This is partly because Browne's proposed free medical care for mothers and children created a Church-State crisis, which brought him into confrontation with the Catholic Church. The hierarchy claimed it was contrary to Catholic social teaching, and because he refused to abandon it, Brown was forced to resign in 1951 as Minister for Health. In 1986 Dr Browne's revealing autobiography, *Against the Tide*, written from his home in Connemara, broke all Irish publishing records. Painted in 1985, this portrait is one of Ballagh's finest works, his mature style demonstrated in clean, spare lines. The meticulous painting of the grey stones in the picture, is continued in real life with a small heap of real stones which spill onto the floor, stressing the connection between art and life. The book titles refer to Karl Marx and Samuel Beckett, whom Browne greatly admired, and the artist's own signature is written in Irish. Choosing to use a limited bright palette, the artist has produced an excellent likeness of a significant and controversial Irishman.

Robert Ballagh was born in Dublin in 1943. He studied architecture at Bolton Street College of Technology until he gave it up to join a pop group. He decided to become a painter, and with no formal art training burst onto the Irish scene with pop-art images and commentaries on the Troubles in Northern Ireland. He contributed to the Irish Exhibition of Living Art, ROSC, and the *Irish Imagination* exhibitions. Since the 1960s he has consistently been one of the most imaginative, sophisticated and inspiring of Irish painters, a brilliant self-publicist, who desires to de-mystify art production. The accomplished photo-realist technique displayed in his paintings is the result of a disciplined work routine. His first one-man exhibition was in 1969 in Dublin and his work has since been acclaimed at home and abroad. Ballagh is also a graphic designer, photographer and designer of stage sets. He is informed by Marxist art theory and consciously attempts to broaden his creative output by producing designs for postage stamps, book covers, sets for contemporary dance productions, black-and-white prints for the Architectural Archive, film titles and Irish bank notes. Ballagh's acclaimed portrait celebrates one of the most important twentieth-century Irish public figures.

Discover Irish Art through the Centuries

18th CENTURY		
Wright, John Michael	c.1617-94	Though born in London, this Scottish artist visited Dublin in 1679 when he painted *The Ladies Catherine and Charlotte Talbot*. During his time in Ireland he painted pictures of a number of aristocratic families.
Morphy, Garret	c.1650-1716	One of the earliest known Irish artists. Morphy was skilled at painting portraits and costume. His portraits were particularly favoured by Jacobite families in Dublin.
Jervas, Charles	c.1675-1739	An accomplished artist who used pastel and pencil as well as oils. He moved between England and Ireland, securing portrait commissions in both countries. In 1727 he became Painter to George II.
Latham, James	1696-1747	Latham became the finest early-eighteenth-century Irish portraitist. He executed single and double portraits, such as *Bishop Robert Clayton and his Wife Katherine*.
Delany, Mary	1700-88	An English-born artist who lived in Ireland between 1743 and 1768. She executed topographical watercolours of some noted gardens, buildings and landscapes. Her eventful life spanned most of the eighteenth century.
Frye, Thomas	1710-62	An oil painter and mezzotint engraver who also used pastel, crayon and watercolours for his portraits.
Hussey, Philip	1713-83	This Cork-born artist led an adventurous life, involving shipwrecks. Many works are known by the artist who painted members of some of the well-known families in south-west Ireland.
Hone the Elder, Nathaniel	1718-84	Dublin-born portrait painter in miniature and oils who was one of the finest painters Ireland has produced. A founder member of the Royal Academy, Hone was a successful and fashionable portraitist and subject painter in London.
Carver, Robert	c.1730-91	His main career was as a scene painter in London, however, he also exhibited a series of landscapes in watercolour and oils.
Barret, George	1732-84	A major landscape painter before he moved to London, where he had a successful and lucrative practice painting landscape views and romantic scenery.

Discover Irish Art through the Centuries

Hamilton, Hugh Douglas	c.1739-1808	A distinguished artist who was successful in Dublin, London and Rome. An acclaimed portrait painter in oil and pastels, he was also known for his historical subjects.
Lewis, John	fl.1740-69	The artist worked as a scene painter at Dublin's Smock Alley Theatre. He painted portraits of a number of theatre people, including the actress Peg Woffington.
Grogan, Nathaniel	c.1740-1807	Despite the fact that this Cork-born artist was self-taught, he produced some of the finest landscapes of the late eighteenth century and some competent genre pictures.
Barry, James	1741-1806	Barry was befriended by Edmund Burke, who financed his studies in Italy. He was a prominent eighteenth-century portaitist and painter of history subjects in the grand-manner in London.
Hickey, Thomas	c.1741-1824	An accomplished portrait painter who spent the years 1784-1824 in India, with one visit home in 1792-98. In addition to oils, he executed charcoal and pastel portraits, and whole-length portrait drawings and sketches.
Dixon, Samuel	c.1745-69	Noted for his important series of embossed pictures, issued in sets of twelve, each one containing a description of a flower or bird and an individual dedication.
Ashford, William	c.1746-1824	An English-born artist who settled in Dublin where he became one of the foremost landscape painters of his time. He became the first President of the Royal Hibernian Academy in 1823.
Wheatley, Francis	1747-1801	A London-born artist who, during the four years he visited Ireland, painted *The Volunteers Meeting in College Green 1779*, representing a unique record of an historical event.
Roberts, Thomas	1748-78	The most gifted eighteenth-century Irish landscape artist, whose *Ideal Landscape*, based on classical-inspired Claudian models and Dutch art, is one of the finest landscapes of the period.
Cunningham, Patrick	fl.1750-74	Of the few works known by this Irish sculptor who trained under Van Nost, the majority are portrait busts carved in a vigorous style that gives the sitter a down-to-earth, pleasing quality. Garden ornamentation formed part of his trade.

Discover Irish Art through the Centuries

Blackburn, Joseph	fl.1752-78	This artist was probably trained in London but first came to prominence in America. An intrepid traveller, he visited Ireland in 1760-67 when be painted a record of the Dublin Lottery.
Hone, Horace	c.1756-1825	The second son of Nathaniel Hone the Elder, he was born in London and came to Ireland in 1782. Appointed miniature-painter to the Prince of Wales in 1795, he was considered the best Irish miniaturist of the period.
Roberts, Thomas Sautelle	1760-1826	A landscape painter in oils, and a master of small-scale watercolour views, his aquatints of Irish scenery are some of the most prized eighteenth-century prints.
Malton, James	c.1760-1803	An English-born artist who was in Dublin between 1785 and 1791. He produced the finest topographical views of Dublin ever made in watercolour and gouache between 1792 and 1799, called *A Picturesque and Descriptive View of the City of Dublin.*
Fisher, Jonathan	fl.1763-1809	A competent landscape painter, many of his topographical views were engraved, such as Killarney (1770), Carlingford (1772) and sixty plates of the Scenery of Ireland (1796).
West, Francis Robert	c.1749-1809	The son of Robert West, first Master at the Dublin Society Drawing Schools. Like his father, he excelled as a draughtsman, particularly in pastel. He exhibited at the Irish Society of Artists 1770-1801, and succeeded to the Mastership of the Schools in 1771.

19th CENTURY

Buck, Adam	1759-1833	The leading nineteenth-century exponent of small, whole-length, neo-classical portraits, usually set against a landscape background. The sculptural feel of the figures reflects the artist's preoccupation with Greek vase painting.
Comerford, John	c.1762-c.1832	This Kilkenny-born portraitist turned from full-scale portraiture to establish himself as one of the most successful miniature painters, and he obtained all his commissions in Ireland.
Mulvany, John George	c.1766-1838	The artist is chiefly remembered as a competent painter of landscape. On the establishment of the RHA in 1823 Mulvany was invited to become a founder member.

Discover Irish Art through the Centuries

Archer Shee, Martin	1769-1850	A celebrated Irish portrait painter of the British aristocracy, he also executed subject pictures on literary, biblical and classical themes. In 1830 he became President of the Royal Academy in London.
Kirk, Thomas	1781-1845	A sculptor who created some elaborate memorials, he is best remembered for the small-scale reliefs on numerous church monuments throughout Ireland.
Sadler, William II	c.1782-1839	Although Sadler's father was a portrait painter, William Sadler II is chiefly known for his small, accurate and unpretentious views of Dublin city and its surroundings, executed on mahogany panels.
Mulready, William	1786-1863	This Ennis-born artist settled in London where he became a successful painter of genre subject pictures and landscapes. His pastel landscape studies and drawings, mostly of figure and genre scenes, are outstanding.
Petrie, George	1790-1866	The most significant nineteenth-century Irish topographical artist who painted views of Ireland in watercolour. He was also a noted antiquary, archaeologist, collector of music and folklore.
Brocas, Samuel Frederick	1792-1847	Arguably the best known of the artistic Brocas family. His twelve famous street views of Dublin dating from 1817 are full of life, anecdotal detail and interest.
O'Connor, James Arthur	1792-1841	An artist best known as an oil painter of romantic landscapes, he also made drawings and watercolours on sketching tours, which formed the basis of his oil paintings.
Danby, Francis	1793-1861	A highly accomplished painter, he spent most of his career in England. His pictures reflect the impact of the Romantic movement on nineteenth-century painting.
Haverty, Joseph P.	1794-1864	A successful Galway-born portrait painter, who also painted narrative Irish subject pictures with religious and nationalistic overtones.
Murphy, Edward	c.1796-1841	Little is known about this accomplished nineteenth-century painter of still life and flower pieces, who also executed caricatures and occasional landscapes.
MacDowell, Patrick	1799-1870	A popular sculptor in his own lifetime, he had a reputation for producing portrait busts and finely designed figures full of touching sentiment.

Discover Irish Art through the Centuries

Hogan, John	1800-58	The most classically inspired of nineteenth-century Irish sculptors. During a career in Rome he returned to Ireland from time to time, receiving commissions for busts, memorials and statues.
Nicholl, Andrew	1804-86	A Belfast-born artist, he was famous for his landscapes and flower-pieces in watercolour. He made illustrations mostly of antiquities, and also taught drawing in Dublin.
Maclise, Daniel	1806-70	A Cork-born artist who did portraits and book illustrations in London. Known primarily as an oil painter, he also worked in pencil and watercolour throughout his career. He executed frescoes for the Houses of Parliament in London and became the most successful history painter of his day.
Mahony, James	1810-79	He was well known for his illustrations of the Famine, which appeared in the *London Illustrated News*. His watercolours vary from landscape and townscape to subject pictures and illustrations.
McManus, Henry	c.1810-78	Working mainly in oil and watercolour, he painted portraits and topographical views. Also an illustrator. His picture *Reading 'The Nation'* is an important record of a paper instrumental in alerting Irish people to issues of Irish national identity.
Davis, William	1812-73	An Irish-born artist who established himself in Liverpool. While initially noted for his portraits and still life, he later turned to landscape, returning to paint occasionally around Leixlip, Co. Kildare.
Burton, Frederic William	1816-1900	The most accomplished nineteenth-century Irish watercolourist, who painted portrait miniatures, genre subject pictures and landscapes. A noted antiquary and art historian, he abandoned painting in 1874 to become Director of the National Gallery, London.
Foley, John Henry	1818-74	Although an Irish artist, Foley was recognised as the finest sculptor of his day in England, executing many commissions of portrait busts and public statuary.
Hayes, Edwin	1820-1904	A Bristol-born marine painter who first worked from a boat sailing between Dublin and Cork. He was a competent artist, who worked for a time as a scene painter in London. His output includes marine subjects in oil and watercolour.
Hayes, Michael Angelo	1820-77	This artist specialised as a painter of horses and military subject matter. A talented draughtsman, he was also accomplished in oils and watercolour.

Discover Irish Art through the Centuries

Barter, Richard	c.1824-96	This Irish-born sculptor's best-known work is a portrait bust in bronze of the statesman Charles Stewart Parnell (1846-91), which he sculpted from photographs. It is signed and dated 1893.
Nicol, Erskine	1825-1904	A Scottish-born artist who spent four years working in Ireland between 1846 and 1850. His Irish works explore the social life of the country, often in a humorous and satirical manner.
Farrell, Thomas	1827-1900	The most prominent sculptor to work in Dublin in the late nineteenth century, his most successful pieces reveal him to be an artist of talent, grace and charm.
Fowler, Trevor T.	fl.1829-44	Little is known about this artist whose output included portraits, subject pictures and views of parts of Munster in the south of Ireland.
Hone the Younger, Nathaniel	1831-1917	A significant Irish landscape painter who spent seventeen years with the Barbizon painters in France. His immediate and fresh landscapes in oil and watercolour provide a unique record of North County Dublin.
Osborne, William	1823-1901	Regarded as one of the finest animal painters of the nineteenth century, particularly in his individual portraits of horses and dogs.
Lawless, Matthew	1837-64	Lawless enjoyed reasonable success as a painter and illustrator although his short life was plagued by illness. *The Sick Call* is the only painting known by him now.
Yeats, John B.	1839-1922	An artist, orator and writer, he was educated as a barrister and took up painting late in life. Yeats was one of the leading portrait painters of his generation. Father of a talented family: William, the poet and dramatist, Lily and Lolly, founders of the Dun Emer and Cuala Press Industries, and Jack, the greatest twentieth-century Irish painter.
Purser, Sarah	1848-1943	She was best known as a portrait painter in oil, pencil, crayon and charcoal, and used watercolour for landscapes. A great patron of the arts in Ireland, she was a founder of the stained-glass studio, An Túr Gloine, and the Friends of the National Collections of Ireland.
Moynan, Richard T.	1856-1906	Having abandoned medicine to train as an artist he established his reputation as a portraitist, although his strength is in genre subject pictures depicting everyday scenes. His watercolours, mostly sketches for oil paintings, include some portraits and landscapes.

Discover Irish Art through the Centuries

Kavanagh, Joseph Malachy	1856-1918	An accomplished academic artist closely associated with the RHA who painted in Antwerp, Brittany and Normandy, and also produced watercolours, drawings and etchings. He was noted for his quiet suburban landscapes of Co. Dublin.
Lavery, John	1856-1941	A Belfast-born artist who achieved international renown for his superb society portraits and genre scenes. Both he and Orpen were appointed official war artists in the First World War.
Butler, Mildred Anne	1858-1941	A highly accomplished watercolourist. The subject matter for her paintings was drawn from the countryside and is evocative of her surroundings in Co. Kilkenny.
Osborne, Walter	1859-1903	Osborne's style combines aspects of naturalism with the colour and freedom of impressionism. He established himself as one of Ireland's most gifted painters of portraits, landscape and genre subject pictures, displaying a genuine feeling for humanity.
Thaddeus, Henry Jones	1859-1929	He was an extremely accomplished painter of portraits and genre who travelled throughout Europe, visited Australia and the Middle East, and lived in North Africa and the United States. Justifiably celebrated for his portraits of Pope Leo XIII (1885) and Pius X (1903).
O'Conor, Roderic	1860-1940	Ireland's first Modernist painter who spent his career in Paris and Brittany. An international figure through his association with Gauguin. His oil paintings are denoted by strong brushwork and a marked feeling for pattern. He also executed watercolours and chalk drawings.
20th CENTURY		
Sheppard, Oliver	1864-1941	An accomplished sculptor, his work consists mainly of sculpted portraits and romantic subjects. He also designed some famous monuments to Irish patriots.
Hughes, John	1864-1941	He was one of Ireland's most talented sculptors working at the turn of the century. His reputation for achieving a convincing likeness resulted in many important commissions.
Yeats, Susan Mary (Lily)	1866-1948	Together with her sister Elizabeth Corbet (Lolly), they founded the Dun Emer and Cuala Press Industries. Many of Lily's embroideries were influenced by her brother Jack's designs.

Discover Irish Art through the Centuries

Yeats, Jack B.	1871-1957	He is undoubtedly the best-known Irish painter of the twentieth century. Born in London, the son of John Butler Yeats, his childhood was spent in Sligo, which provided material for his later work. He began working as an illustrator, and painted in watercolour before turning to oils. It was his late great expressive oil paintings that won him an international reputation.
Healy, Michael	1873-1941	An Irish stained-glass artist whose small figure sketches in watercolour faithfully recorded Dubliners. He joined An Túr Gloine in 1903, where he executed many notable windows.
Connor, Jerome	1874-1943	During Connor's long career as a sculptor he lived alternately in America and Ireland, carrying out a series of successful and accomplished commemorative monuments.
Henry, Paul	1876-1958	This Belfast-born oil painter made sketches of Irish people, scenes and landscapes. Most of his paintings are associated with a west of Ireland landscape genre, which was originally developed during his time on Achill Island.
Orpen, William	1878-1931	Best known as a successful, accomplished portrait painter in oils, he was also a superb draughtsman. Although based in London, for over twelve years he travelled to Dublin and taught the next generation of Irish artists.
Power, Albert	1881-1945	During his long career as a sculptor, Power received important commissions, which included portraits of leading literary and political figures of the day.
Leech, William	1881-1968	Acclaimed for his portraits, landscapes and still life, he executed self-portraits, interiors and flower paintings; he is best known for his genre pictures such as *The Convent Garden, Brittany*.
Swanzy, Mary	1882-1978	A champion of modernism in Irish art, she was a noted figure, portrait and landscape painter. Swanzy achieved an international reputation.
Clarke, Margaret	1888-1961	A pupil of Orpen who taught at the Dublin Metropolitan School of Art. She was a meticulous draughtswoman, displaying considerable talent in portrait-painting and also genre subjects.
Clarke, Harry	1889-1931	Undoubtedly one of Ireland's greatest stained-glass artists. He is noted particularly for his windows in the Honan Chapel, Cork. He proved to be equally brilliant as an illustrator of books and a textile designer.

Discover Irish Art through the Centuries

Keating, Seán	1889-1977	A portrait and figure painter who was Professor of Painting at the National College of Art. He was much concerned with national imagery and the creation of a distinctive Irish subject matter in art.
Whelan, Leo	1892-1956	An accomplished portrait painter, who during the 1930s and 1940s was celebrated for his series of portraits of major twentieth-century Irish public figures.
Lamb, Charles	1893-1964	This Northern artist from Portadown is chiefly remembered for his Irish subject pictures, portraits of Connemara people in monumental pose and Carraroe-inspired landscapes and seascapes.
Tuohy, Patrick	1894-1930	A well-known pupil of Orpen. He was a prolific artist whose career spanned landscapes, religious subjects and ceiling paintings. He also produced an accomplished series of literary, artistic and political portraits of the decade.
Hone, Evie	1894-1955	Hone, who was descended from a dynasty of painters, was a highly influential stained-glass artist, also painting pictures in gouache. Her masterpiece, the east window of Eton College Chapel, illustrates her bold expressive style.
Jellett, Mainie	1897-1944	Leader of the Modern Movement in Ireland and founder of the Irish Exhibition of Living Art. Her personal style, based on cubist principles, is denoted by rhythm and movement, colour and form. She worked in oil, gouache and watercolour.
Kernoff, Harry	1900-74	Although born in London, Kernoff became a unique chronicler of Dublin and its ordinary citizens. He developed a highly personal linear style, illustrated in well-known mid-century theatrical personalities, and was also a graphic artist, book illustrator and designer for costume and theatre.
MacGonigal, Maurice	1900-79	An outstanding painter and teacher at the National College of Art. His death marked the end of a generation of artists who were significant in forging a sense of identity for independent Ireland.
O'Sullivan, Seán	1906-64	One of Ireland's most gifted draughtsmen, his reputation rests largely on his small portrait drawings of some major twentieth-century figures in pencil, chalk and pastel.
Van Stockum, Hilda	b.1908	A Dutch artist of Irish descent, known for her superb still-life tempera paintings and her portraits. She is a well-respected writer and illustrator of children's books.

Discover Irish Art through the Centuries

Hanlon, Jack	1913-68	A fine painter of figure compositions and religious subjects, he is justifiably acclaimed for his much-sought-after, delicately coloured watercolours of flowers.
Kelly, Oisín	1915-81	Kelly is renowned for his bronze sculpture in the Garden of Remembrance. While influenced by abstract sculpture, a strain of realism is evident throughout his work.
Hennessy, Patrick	1915-80	Hennessy was a painter of still life, landscape and *trompe-l'oeil* (illusionist painting planned to deceive the eye). He painted in a photo-realist style, paying great attention to detail.
Dillon, Gerard	1916-71	A Belfast-born painter who developed an innocent, child-like, primitive style, well-illustrated in his paintings, etchings, stage sets and designs for murals and tapestries.
Yeats, Anne	b.1919	A painter, illustrator, stage designer and printmaker. An active member of the Irish Exhibition of Living Art since its foundation in 1943, she revived the Cuala Press in the 1970s and presented the Jack B. Yeats Archive to the National Gallery of Ireland.
McGuire, Edward	1932-86	A leading portraitist, his practice was to treat his subjects in a full-frontal, static, stylised manner. Many of his portraits were of well-known literary figures.
Ballagh, Robert	b.1943	Ballagh is a popular contemporary artist whose early Pop-Art imagery gave way to a mature, sophisticated, photo-realist style, illustrated in a series of portraits of well-known twentieth-century figures. He is a successful graphic artist and designer of dance sets.

Bibliography

PRIMARY SOURCES: BOOKS, ARTICLES AND CATALOGUES RELEVANT TO THIS BOOK

BOOKS

ANGLESEA, M. *The Royal Ulster Academy of Arts – A Centennial History*. Royal Ulster Academy of Arts, 1981

ARNOLD, B. *A Concise History of Irish Art*. Thames & Hudson, 1969
    Mainie Jellett and the Modern Movement in Ireland. Yale University Press, 1991
    Orpen: Mirror to an Age. Jonathan Cape, 1991
    Swift: An Illustrated Life. Lilliput Press, 1999

BENCE-JONES, M. *Life in an Irish Country House*. Constable, 1996

BENEZIT, E.C. *Benezit. Dictionnaire Critique et Documentaire des Peintres, Sculpteurs, Dessinateurs et Graveurs*. Nouvelle Edition, Ten vols. Paris, 1976

BENNINGTON, R. *Roderic O'Conor*. Irish Academic Press, 1992

BODKIN, T. *Twelve Irish Artists*. Victor Waddington Publications, 1940
    Four Irish Landscape Painters. Irish Academic Press, 1987

BROWNE, T. *Ireland: A Social and Cultural History 1922-79*. Fontana, 1981

BOURKE, M. *Exploring Art at the National Gallery*. National Gallery of Ireland, 1997
    Art in Transition, National Gallery of Ireland, 1998

BOYLAN, H. *Dictionary of Irish Biography*. ColourBooks Ltd, 1998

BREEZE, G. *Society of Artists in Ireland, Index of Exhibits 1765-80*. National Gallery of Ireland, 1985

BUTLER, P. *Three Hundred Years of Irish Watercolours and Drawings*. Weidenfeld & Nicholson, 1990

CARTY, C. *Robert Ballagh*. Magill, 1986

CATTO, M. *Art in Ulster II*. Blackstaff Press, 1977

COLLINS, T. (Ed.). *Decoding the Landscape*. Centre for Landscape Studies, University College Galway, 1994

CONNOLLY S. J. (Ed.). *The Oxford Companion to Irish History*. Oxford University Press. 1998

COOMBS, K. *The Portrait Miniature in England*. London 1998

CRAIG, M. *Georgian Dublin: Aquatint Views by James Malton*. Dolmen Press, 1985
    Classic Irish Houses of the Middle Size. The Architectural Press, London, 1986

CROOKSHANK, A. *Irish Sculpture from 1600 to the Present Day*. Department of Foreign Affairs, 1984
    Mildred Anne Butler. Town House/National Gallery of Ireland, 1992

CROOKSHANK, A. & The Knight of Glin. *The Painters of Ireland 1660-1920*. Barrie & Jenkins, 1978
    The Watercolours of Ireland. Barrie & Jenkins, 1994

CULLEN, F. *Visual Politics, the Representations of Ireland 1750-1930*. Cork University Press, 1997

DALSIMER, A. *Visualising Ireland, National Identity and the Pictorial Tradition*. Faber & Faber, 1993

DUNLEVY, M. *Dress in Ireland*. Batsford Ltd, 1989

FALLON, B. *Irish Art 1830-1990*. Appletree Press, 1994
    Edward McGuire RHA. Irish Academic Press, 1991
    The Age of Innocence – Irish Culture 1930-60. Gill & Macmillan, 1998

FITZGERALD, D. (The Knight of Glin) *Irish Furniture*. Dublin, 1978

FITZ-SIMON, C. *The Arts in Ireland: A Chronology*. Gill & Macmillan, 1982

FOSTER, R. *Modern Ireland 1600-1972*. Penguin, 1988

FOSTER, R.F. (Ed.) *The Illustrated History of Ireland*. Oxford University Press, 1989

FROST, S. *A Tribute to Evie Hone and Mainie Jellett*. Browne and Nolan Ltd, 1957

GORDON BOWE, N., Caron, D., Wynne, M. *Gazetteer of Irish Stained Glass*. Irish
      Academic Press, 1988
      The Life and Work of Harry Clarke. Irish Academic Press, 1989

GORDON BOWE, N., Cummings, E. *The Arts and Crafts Movement in Dublin and Edinburgh*. Irish
      Academic Press, 1998

GRAVES, A. *The Royal Academy of Arts: A Complete Dictionary of Contributors and their Work from its
      Foundation in 1769 to 1904*. Four vols. Kingsmead Reprints, 1970

GREENACRE, N. *Francis Danby*. Tate Gallery, London, 1988

HARBISON, P., Potterton, H., & Sheehy, J. *Irish Art and Architecture*. Thames & Hudson, 1987

HARBISON, P., O'Brien, J. *Ancient Ireland from Prehistory to the Middle Ages*. Weidenfeld &
      Nicholson, 1996

HARDWICK, J. *The Yeats Sisters*. Pandora/Harper Collins, 1996

HAYDEN, R. *Mrs Delany and Her Flower Collages*. British Museum Press, 1992

HERITY, M., Eoghan G. *Ireland in Prehistory*. Routledge, 1989

HEWITT, J. *Art in Ulster I*. Blackstaff Press, 1977

HILL, J. *Irish Public Sculpture*. Four Courts Press, 1998

INGAMELLS, J. *A Dictionary of British and Irish Travellers in Italy 1701-1800*. Yale University Press, 1997

KELLY, L. *Thinking Long: Contemporary Art in the North of Ireland*. Gandon Publications, 1996

KENNEDY, B. P. *Irish Painting*. Town House and Country House, 1993
      Dreams and Responsibilities: The State and Art in Independent Ireland. The Arts Council, 1990

KENNEDY, B. P. & Gillespie R. (Eds.). *Ireland – Art into History*. Town House and Country
      House, 1994

KENNEDY S. B. *Paul Henry*. Town House/National Gallery of Ireland, 1991
      Irish Art and Modernism 1880-1950. Institute of Irish Studies, Queen's University, 1991

KIBERD, D. *Inventing Ireland: The Literature of a Modern Nation*. Vintage, 1996

LARMOUR, P. *The Arts and Crafts Movement*. Friars Bush Press, 1994

LE HARIVEL, A. *Nathaniel Hone the Elder*. Town House/National Gallery of Ireland, 1992

MACCURTIN, M., O'Corrain, D. *Women in Irish Society: The Historical Dimension*.
      Greenwood Press, 1979

McCONKEY, K. *A Free Spirit, Irish Art 1860-1960*. Antique Collectors Club & Pyms Gallery, 1990
      Sir John Lavery. Cannongate Press, 1993

MCDONNELL, J. *500 Years of the Irish Book – 1500 to the Present*. National Gallery of Ireland, 1997
    Irish Eighteenth-Century Stuccowork and its European Sources. National Gallery of Ireland, 1991

MCPARLAND, E. *James Gandon Vitruvius Hibernicus*. A. Zwemmer Ltd, 1985

MCREDMOND, L. (Ed.). *Modern Irish Lives, A Dictionary of Twentieth-Century Irish Biography*. ColourBooks Ltd, 1999

MARSHALL, C. *Irish Art Masterpieces*. Hugh Lauter Levin Assoc. Inc., 1994

MURPHY, W. M. *The Prodigal Father – The Life of John Butler Yeats 1839-1922*. Cornell University Press, 1979

O'DOWD, A. *Common Clothes and Clothing 1860-1930*. National Museum of Ireland, 1990

O GRÁDA, C. *Black 47 and Beyond: The Great Irish Famine in History, Economy and Memory*. Princeton University Press, 1999

O'GRADY, J. *The Life and Work of Sarah Purser*. Four Courts Press, 1996

PASQUIN, A. *Memoirs of the Royal Academicians and an Authentic History of the Artists in Ireland (1796)*, London 1970

POINTON, M. *Mulready*. Victoria and Albert Museum, 1986

PRESSLY, W. L. *The Life and Art of James Barry*. Yale University Press, 1981

PYLE, H. *Jack B. Yeats: A Biography*. Routledge & Keegan Paul, 1970
    Jack B. Yeats: Catalogue Raisonné of the Oil Paintings. Three vols. André Deutsch, 1992
    Jack B. Yeats: The Watercolours, Drawings and Pastels. Irish Academic Press, 1993
    Yeats: Portrait of an Artistic Family. National Gallery of Ireland, 1997

SHEEHY, J. *The Rediscovery of Ireland's Past – The Celtic Revival 1830-1930*. Thames & Hudson, 1980
    Walter Osborne. Town House/National Gallery of Ireland, 1991

SNODDY, T. *A Dictionary of Irish Artists in the Twentieth Century*. Wolfhound Press, 1996

SOMERVILLE-LARGE, P. *The Irish Country House: A Social History*. Sinclair-Stevenson, 1995

STAIRS, S. *The Irish Figurists and Figurative Painting in Irish Art*. The George Gallery Montague Ltd, 1990

STEWARD, J. (Ed.), *When Time Began to Rant and Rage: Figurative Painting from Twentieth-Century Ireland*. University of California, Berkeley Art Museum, 1998

STEWART, A. *Royal Hibernian Academy of Arts; Index of Exhibitors 1826-1976*. Manton Publishers, Vol 1 1985, Vol 2 1986, Vol 3 1987
    Irish Art Loan Exhibitions 1765-1927, Index of Artists. JAP & Manton Publishing, 1990
    Irish Societies and Sketching Clubs 1870-1980. Fourcourt Press, 1997

STOKES, W. *The Life and Labours in Art and Archaeology of George Petrie*. London, 1868

STRICKLAND, W. *A Dictionary of Irish Artists*. Two vols. 1913. Reprinted Irish Academic Press, 1989

TURPIN, J. *A School of Art in Dublin since the Eighteenth Century*. Gill and Macmillan, 1995
    John Hogan, Irish Neo-classical Sculptor in Rome. Irish Academic Press, 1982

WEBSTER, M. *Francis Wheatley*. Paul Mellon Foundation for British Art, 1970

WHITE, J. *Gerard Dillon. An Illustrated Biography.* Wolfhound Press, 1994
WYNNE, M. *Fifty Irish Painters.* National Gallery of Ireland, 1983

ARTICLES

ADAMS, R. 'Andrew Nicholl.' *Irish Arts Review,* Vol 1, No. 4, 1984

ALLEN, G. 'Seán Keating Regrets.' *The Irish Press,* 20 October 1977

ARCHER, M.A. 'Wellington and South India: Portraits by Thomas Hickey.' *Apollo,* Vol 1 & 2, No. 161, 1975

BAILEY, C. 'Matthew James Lawless.' *Irish Arts Review,* Vol 4, No. 2, 1987

BARRETT, C. 'Irish Nationalism and Art.' *Studies,* (winter) 1975

BHREATHNACH-LYNCH, S. 'Albert Power RHA.' *Irish Arts Review Yearbook,* Vol 7, 1990/91
  'John Hughes: The Italian Connection.' *Irish Arts Review Yearbook,* Vol 10, 1994.
  'The Irish Collection in the National Gallery.' *Éire/Ireland,* Vol xxxiii, Nos. 2 & 3, 1998

BLACK, E. 'The Royal Irish Art Union 1839-59.' *Irish Arts Review Yearbook.* Vol 14, 1998

BOURKE, M. 'The Aran Fisherman's Drowned Child by Frederic William Burton RHA.' *Irish Arts Review Yearbook,* Vol 5, 1988
  'Frederic William Burton; Painter, Antiquarian and Art Historian.' *Éire-Ireland.* Journal of Irish Studies, Minnesota, 1991
  'Portrait of Evie Hone in her Studio by Hilda van Stockum.' *Studies.* Summer 1997

BRIGGS, C. 'Margaret Clarke RHA 1888-1961.' *Allegemeines Kunstlerlexikon,* Vol C, 1998

BUTLER, P. 'The Ingenious Francis Place.' *Irish Arts Review,* Vol 1, No. 4, 1984

CAFFREY, P. 'John Comerford.' *Irish Arts Review,* Vol 4, No. 3, 1987
  'Samuel Lover's Achievements as a Painter.' *Irish Arts Review,* Vol 3, No. 1, 1986

CASEY, C. 'A Wax Bas-Relief by Patrick Cunningham.' *Irish Arts Review Yearbook,* Vol. 11, 1995

COLEMAN, J. 'A Painter of Living Art: Jack P. Hanlon.' *Irish Arts Review Yearbook,* Vol 5, 1988/89

CROFTS, S. 'Maurice MacGonigal PHRA and his Western Paintings.' *Irish Arts Review Yearbook,* Vol 13, 1997

CRONIN, M., O'Connor, B. (Eds.) 'Embodying the Nation – The West of Ireland Landscape and Irish Identity.' *Tourism in Ireland/A Critical Analysis.* Cork University Press 1993

CROOKSHANK, A. 'James Latham 1696-1747.' *Irish Arts Review Yearbook,* Vol 5, 1988/89
  'A Life devoted to Landscape Painting – William Ashford c.1746-1824.' *Irish Arts Review Yearbook,* Vol 11, 1995

CROOKSHANK, A. & The Knight of Glin. 'Some Italian Pastels by Hugh Douglas Hamilton.' *Irish Arts Review Yearbook,* Vol 13, 1997

CRUICKSHANK, J G. 'Grace Henry.' *Irish Arts Review Yearbook,* Vol 9, 1993

CULLEN, F. 'Hugh Douglas Hamilton in Rome 1779-92.' *Apollo,* Vol 115, 1982

FFOLLIOTT, R. 'Fashion as a Guide to Dating Irish Portraits 1660-1880.' *Irish Arts Review Yearbook*, 1989-90

FENLON, J. 'Garret Morphy and his Circle.' *Irish Arts Review Yearbook*, Vol 8, 1991/2

FIGGIS, N. 'Irish Landscapists in Rome 1750-80.' *Irish Arts Review*, Vol. 4, No. 4, 1987
'Irish Artists and Society in Eighteenth-Century Rome.' *Irish Arts Review*, Vol. 3, No. 3, 1986
'Irish Portrait and Subject Painters in Rome 1750-1800.' *Irish Arts Review Yearbook*, Vol. 5, 1988

FOWLER, J. 'Art and Independence: An Aspect of Twentieth-Century Irish Art.' *Circa*, (Jan/Feb) 1984

HARTIGAN, M. 'The Irish Exhibition of Living Art.' *Irish Arts Review*, Vol 4, No. 4, 1987

JENKINS, I. 'Adam Buck and the Vogue for Greek Vases.' *The Burlington Magazine*. Vol. CXXX, No. 1023

JENKNER, I. 'Portrait or Genre? Mary and Brigid by Margaret Clarke.' *Irish Arts Review Yearbook*, Vol 15, 1999

KELLY, F. 'The Life and Works of Oisín Kelly.' *Irish Arts Review Yearbook*. Vol 6, 1989/90

KENNEDY, B. P. 'Irish Landscape Painting in a Political Setting 1922-48.' *Aspects of Irish Studies*, Belfast, 1990

KENNEDY, M. 'Robert Ballagh.' *The Irish Times*, 30 July 1997

LAFFAN, W. 'Taste, Elegance and Execution: John Lewis as a Landscape Painter.' *Irish Arts Review Yearbook*, Vol 15, 1999

LENEHAN, P. 'Edward Smyth, Dublin's Sculptor.' *Irish Arts Review Yearbook*, Vol 6, 1989/90

MARSHALL, C. 'Choosing the Battleground, Robert Ballagh's Painting.' *Irish Arts Review Yearbook*, Vol 12, 1996

MULCAHY, R. 'Patrick J. Tuohy 1894-1903.' *Irish Arts Review Yearbook*, Vol 6, 1989/90

MURPHY, P. 'John Henry Foley's O'Connell Monument.' *Irish Arts Review Yearbook*, Vol 11, 1995
'Thomas Farrell, Sculptor.' *Irish Arts Review Yearbook*, Vol 9, 1993

O'BRIEN, K. 'Harry Kernoff RHA.' *Martello*, Spring 1990

O'CONNOR, A. 'James Latham: Two Portraits.' *Burlington Magazine*. Vol 116, No. 852, 1974

POTTERTON, H. 'A Director with Distinction.' *Country Life*, 1974

RYAN SMOLIN, W. 'Leo Whelan 1892 – 1956.' *Irish Arts Review Yearbook*, Vol 10, 1994
'William Sadler's Views of Killua Castle, Co. Westmeath.' *Irish Arts Review Yearbook*, Vol 12, 1996

SHEEHY, J. 'The Irish at Antwerp.' *Irish Arts Review Yearbook*, Vol 10, 1994

TURPIN, J. 'Oliver Sheppard's 1987 Memorial in Co. Wexford.' *Irish Arts Review Yearbook*, Vol 7, 1990/1

'The Royal Hibernian Academy Schools: The First Eighty Years (1826-1906).' *Irish Arts Review Yearbook*, Vol 8, 1991/2

'The Education of Irish Artists 1877-1975.' *Irish Arts Review Yearbook*, Vol 13, 1997

WYNNE, M. 'Continental European Sources for George Barret 1728/32-84.' *Irish Arts Review Yearbook*, Vol 10, 1994

'Thomas Roberts 1748-78.' *Irish Arts Review Yearbook*, Vol 10, 1994

'Thomas Frye.' *Burlington Magazine*, London, Vol 124, 1982

CATALOGUES

BENEDETTI, S. *The La Touche Amorino. Canova and his Fashionable Patrons*. National Gallery of Ireland, 1998

The Milltowns, A Family Reunion. National Gallery of Ireland, 1997

BOURKE, M. *Charles Lamb RHA: Galway Paintings*. Galway Arts Centre, 1998

Painting in Focus: Frederic William Burton's 'The Aran Fisherman's Drowned Child'. Touring Exhibition Services, 1987

BRENNAN, F. *Mary Swanzy 1882-1978*. Pyms Gallery, London, 1986

BUTLER, P. *The Brocas Collection*. National Library of Ireland, 1997

CAFFREY, P. *John Comerford and The Portrait Miniature in Ireland c.1620-1850*. Kilkenny Archaeological Society, 1999

CAMPBELL, J. *The Irish Impressionists in Ireland, France and Belgium*. National Gallery of Ireland, 1984

Onlookers in France: Irish Realist and Impressionist Painters. Crawford Municipal Art Gallery, Cork, 1993

Nathaniel Hone the Younger. National Gallery of Ireland, 1992

Irish Artists in Brittany. Musée de Pont Aven and The Crawford Municipal Art Gallery, Cork, 1999

Mary Swanzy 1882-1978. Pyms Gallery, London, 1986

CASEY, C. *Folk Tradition in Irish Art*. Collection of the Department of Folklore. University College Dublin, 1993

CORK ART SOCIETY. *Tribute to Patrick Hennessy*. Cork Arts Society, 1981

CROKE, F., Keaveney, R., Kennedy, B. P., Le Harivel, A., Wynne, M. *Irish Watercolours and Drawings*. National Gallery of Ireland/Boston College, 1991

CROUAN, C. *Maurice MacGonigal*. Hugh Lane Municipal Gallery of Modern Art, Dublin, 1991

DALSIMER, A., Kreilkamp, V. *America's Eye: Irish Paintings from the Collection of Brian Burns*. Boston College Museum of Art, 1996

FERRAN, D. *Leech: An Irish Painter Abroad*. National Gallery of Ireland, 1996

GRAEVE, J. (Ed). *In a State, An Exhibition in Kilmainham Gaol on National Identity*. Project Press, 1991

HOBART, M. *The Irish Revival.* Pyms Gallery, London 1982

HODGE, A. *NCAD 250 Drawings 1746-1996.* National College of Art and Design, *1996*

HUTCHINSON, J. *James Arthur O'Connor.* National Gallery of Ireland, 1985

JOHNSTON, R. *Roderic O'Conor 1860-1940.* Barbican Art Gallery, London, 1985

LE HARIVEL, A. *Illustrated Summary Catalogue of Drawings, Watercolours and Miniatures.* National Gallery of Ireland, 1983
 Frederic William Burton. National Gallery of Ireland, 1997

LE HARIVEL, A. (Ed). *Illustrated Summary Catalogue of Prints and Sculpture.* National Gallery of Ireland, 1988

LE HARIVEL, A., Hutchinson, J., Wynne, M. *Illustrated Summary Catalogue of Paintings.* National Gallery of Ireland, 1981

LE HARIVEL, A. and GOACHER, M. *Two Hundred Years of Watercolours.* National Gallery of Ireland, 1997

MACGONIGAL, C. *Harry Kernoff.* Hugh Lane Municipal Gallery of Modern Art, Dublin, 1976.

McCONKEY, K. *Irish Renascence, Irish Art in a Century of Change.* Pyms Gallery, London, 1986

McMONAGLE, A. (Ed.) *Seán Keating and the ESB.* Touring Exhibition Services, 1987

MURPHY, A. *The Paintings of Paul and Grace Henry.* Hugh Lane Municipal Gallery of Modern Art, Dublin, 1991

MURRAY, P. (Ed.). *Irish Art 1779-1995 History and Society.* Crawford Municipal Art Gallery. Cork VEC, 1997

O'CONNELL, D. *Mainie Jellett.* Irish Museum of Modern Art, 1991

Ó MURCHÚ, G. *Jerome Connor Irish American Sculptor 1874-1943.* National Gallery of Ireland, 1993

RUANE, F. *The Allied Irish Banks Collection of Twentieth-Century Irish Art.* Douglas Hyde Gallery, Dublin, 1986

RYAN SMOLIN, W., Mayes, E., & Rogers, J. (Eds). *Irish Women Artists.* National Gallery of Ireland, 1987

SHEEHY, J. *Walter Osborne.* National Gallery of Ireland, 1983

SHERWOOD, M. *Ireland and the Modern Movement.* Taylor Gallery, London, 1990

STEVENSON, S., Thompson, D. *John Michael Wright: The King's Painter.* Scottish National Portrait Gallery, 1982

TURPIN, J. & Ormond, R. *Daniel Maclise 1808-70.* Arts Council of Great Britain, 1972

WALKER, R. *Miniatures: 300 Years of the English Miniature Illustrated from the Collections of the National Portrait Collection.* National Portrait Gallery, London, 1998

WHITE, J. *Seán Keating PRHA 1889-1977.* Royal Hibernian Academy Gallagher Gallery, 1989
 Evie Hone. The Municipal Gallery, Dublin, 1958

WYNNE, M. *The MacNeill Sweeney Bequest. Acquisitions 1984-86.* National Gallery of Ireland, 1986.

Index of Artists

Note: *This index refers to the notes on the artists that accompany the illustrated works. For other references to the artists, see the General Index.*

Index of Works

Note: *This index refers to the one hundred works illustrated in colour. For other works mentioned in the text, see the General Index.*

General Index